REV. FR

LIBERALISM & CATHOLICISM

PROPERTY OF
SAINT JOSEPH LIBRARY

Translated and adapted from French by
Rev. Fr. Coenraad Daniels
Professor at Holy Cross Seminary (Society of Saint Pius X), Goulburn, Australia.

ANGELUS PRESS
2918 TRACY AVENUE, KANSAS CITY, MISSOURI 64109

Nihil obstat Die 12th mensis Augusti
Censor deputatus,
H. Mottais.

Imprimatur

die 28 mensis Augusti 1926

☩ Alexius-Armandus Cardinalis Charost,
Archiep, Rhedonensis.

©1998 by Angelus Press
All rights reserved. No part of this book may be reproduced or transmitted in any form or by any means, electronic or mechanical, including photocopying, recording, or by any information storage and retrieval systems without permission in writing from the publisher except by a reviewer who may quote brief passages in a review.

ANGELUS PRESS
2918 Tracy Avenue
Kansas City, Missouri 64109
Phone (816) 753-3150
Fax (816) 753-3557
Order Line 1-800-966-7337

ISBN 0-935952-53-5
FIRST PRINTING—April 1998

Printed in the United States of America

Admonition

The book you are about to read is a set of conferences presented to the *Semaine Catholique* in February, 1926, by Rev. Fr. A. Roussel (Doctor of Philosophy, Professor of the Major Seminary of Rennes, France). These and other similar conferences were given under the auspices of the Apostolic League for the Return of Nations to the Christian Order.

These have now been translated from the original French and adapted to the English reader by Rev. Fr. C. Daniels, priest of The Society of Saint Pius X.

Feast of St. Ignatius of Loyola
July 31, 1996
Goulburn, Australia

PREFACE

Archbishop Lefebvre called it the *"great betrayal"*.[1] He was speaking of Catholic liberalism, the attempt to reconcile the Church with the revolution. He explains himself:

>...there is in liberal Catholicism (a term that I use with repugnance, because it is a blasphemy) a betrayal of the principles which it disavows, a practical apostasy of the Faith in the social kingship of Our Lord Jesus Christ.[2]

It is the development of liberalism and its progressive infiltration into the Catholic Church which Fr. Roussel's book traces for us. This phenomenon, which began with the French Revolution of 1789 and progressed throughout the 19th century, engendering modernism at the beginning of the 20th century, is of the utmost importance for us at the end of the 20th century. It has now brought forth its bitter fruits, the destruction of the whole order of society, as Pope Gregory XVI predicted in 1832:

>Thence, in fact, the instability of minds; thence the ever increasing corruption of the young; thence, in the people, the contempt of sacred rights and holiest laws and things; thence, in a word, the saddest scourge that can ravage States, since experience attests, and the remotest antiquity teaches, that cities powerful in wealth, dominion, and glory perished by this sole evil—the unbridled liberty of opinions, the license of public discourse, the passion for changes.[3]

This is precisely what we are witnessing at the end of this 20th century. The Church having been engulfed by liberalism, society is now falling apart.

We are very grateful, indeed, for Fr. Daniel's making this text available to us in English. For it is impossible to comprehend the crisis in the post-conciliar church, and the radical transformation attempted in the name of progress since Vatican II, without

---

[1] Archbishop Marcel Lefebvre, *They Have Uncrowned Him* (Kansas City: Angelus Press, 1988), p.107.
[2] *Ibid.* p.109
[3] Pope Gregory XVI, *Mirari Vos* (Kansas City: Angelus Press), no.15, p.12.

understanding the liberal mindset which prepared the way. This book is consequently indispensable for any student of the history of the crisis in the Church or of Vatican II. It is likewise crucial for us to read and absorb if we are to know how to react to post-conciliar liberalism, that is if we are to have the strength of conviction to refuse all compromise with the attack on the supernatural Catholic Faith that it really is.

The importance of this book can be measured by these words of Archbishop Lefebvre:

> Yes, truly, Vatican Council II is the ratification of liberal Catholicism. And when it is remembered that Pope Pius IX, 85 years earlier, said and repeated to those who were visiting him in Rome; "Be careful! There are no worse enemies of the Church than the liberal Catholics!"—then can be measured the catastrophe that such liberal Popes and such a council represent for the Church and for the reign of Our Lord Jesus Christ![4]

Reverend Fr. Peter R. Scott

---

[4] Archbishop Marcel Lefebvre, *They Have Uncrowned Him* (Kansas City: Angelus Press, 1988), p.222.

TABLE OF CONTENTS

PART I

LIBERALISM IN GENERAL

Introduction 1
Interpretation of the Term "Liberal" 1
The True Notion of Liberty 3
Aspects of Liberalism. Its Definition 6

Chapter I: Origin of Liberalism, Historical Developments, Actual State of Affairs 11
First Origins 11
Protestantism—Luther 12
Naturalism and Rationalism 13
    Notion and Definition 13
    The "Separated" Philosophy: Descartes, Kant, Cousin 14
    "Philosophism" : Bayle, Diderot, Voltaire 15
    Revolutionary Philosophy: Rousseau, the Revolution 16
    Romanticism: Mme. Stael, Chateaubriand,
        Michelet, Victor Hugo 18
    Modern Liberalism: Tolstoy, Jaurès, Buisson 18

Chapter II: Logical Development and Synthesis of Liberalism 21
In General Philosophy 22
In Religion and Morality 23

Chapter III: Political and Social Liberalism 27
Civil Society—The State according to Liberalism 28
Universal Secularism 30
The War against the Catholic Hierarchy...................... 31
An Historical Sketch on Political and Social Liberalism............... 32

Chapter IV: The Refutation of Liberalism: "Secular" Faith or Catholic Faith 37
The Autonomy of Man—Liberty of Conscience 37
Catholic Truth—Liberal Error 40

Conclusion 45

PART II

"CATHOLIC" OR PRACTICAL LIBERALISM

Introduction: Diverse Forms of Liberalism 49

Chapter I: Origin and Development of "Catholic Liberalism" 51
The Expression "Catholic Liberalism" 51
Felicite de Lamennais 52
The "Liberal-Catholic" School 54

Chapter II: The "Liberal Catholic" Mentality............... 57
What a "Liberal Catholic" is and What He is Not....... 57
The Profound Incoherency of "Liberal Catholicism" 63
The "Liberal Catholic" in the Speculative Order 64
The Liberal Catholic in General Practice...................... 68
    Desire for Peace 68
    Charitable Attitude 70
    Prudent Conduct 71

A Sense of Reality 71
Falseness of Mind 73
The "Liberal Catholic" Journal 76

Chapter III: The Relations of Church and State According to the "Liberal Catholic" 81

The Catholic Doctrine—The Divine Plan 81
The Practice According to History 83
The Attitude of the "Liberal Catholic"—The Thesis
and the Hypothesis 84
    a) He Separates the theory and practice 88
    *b) The "Liberal Catholic" attributes only a
    theoretical value to the teachings of the Church* 94
    *c) Regarding tolerance. The "Liberal Catholic"
    confuses the duties of the chiefs of State
    and those of the Catholic citizen* 94
    *d) The "Liberal Catholic" freely imagines
    the Christian right to be a pure myth* 95
Separation of the Public and Private Domains 96
The Democratic Ambiguity 102

Conclusion 109

The Danger of "Liberal Catholicism" 109
Remedies to "Liberal Catholicism" 125
More Positive Remedies 125
Dangers and Abuse of Words 133

PART I

LIBERALISM IN GENERAL

INTRODUCTION

May Our Lord Jesus Christ, Son of God and Redeemer of mankind, reign over every individual, family, over nations and over the entire social order. There is no greater adversary of the social kingship of Jesus Christ, so necessary for all, than modern Liberalism due to its audacity, tenaciousness and influence.

What is Liberalism? Where does it come from? By which principles is it manifested, and how does it logically develop? How do we explain it, and how do we refute it? These are some of the many questions to which we would like to reply.

Interpretation of the Term "Liberal"

The term "liberal" as also the term "liberty," from which it comes, pleases the unthinking masses because of its vagueness. It sounds so easy to the ear, and, what is more, allows each to interpret it according to his own liking, convictions, sentiments and interests. It lends itself to ambiguities, and consequentially, becomes extremely dangerous.

On the one hand, it is conformable to the free man, on the other, to a sensitive, pious and generous heart. It is according to the last sense, that God is, as St. Thomas explains, *maxime liberalis*.[1] This term, however, also lends itself to the "love of a certain liberty." This last is to which we are referring. The Liberal is he who declares himself a partisan of liberty. We will,

---

[1] *Summa Theologica*, I, Q.44, A.4, ad.1.

however, encounter many different ways of being "liberal," each according to diverse interpretations of the word "liberty."

The liberal party could include, for example, the disciples of Voltaire and Rousseau, absolutely imbued with the principles of the French Revolution of 1789. They declared themselves absolute enemies of the Catholic Church and any form of monarchy, following with great devotion the "modern liberties" conceived as a definite conquering of any thing that might even smell of authority.

Then one would move to a more "mitigated" form under the influence of a certain French priest of the last century, by the name of Félicité de Lamennais. One would then be praised with the name of "modern libertines." These would be the fervent disciples of the Declaration of the Rights of Man, who would claim to have the monopoly on "integral Liberalism." The "Liberals" of 1789 would then become the "Radicals." Finally, today, the term "liberal" is applied as a title of honor to every mind and system that may be favorable to any liberty accepted as a norm at any given moment.

We will endeavor to help the reader understand the clear and pejorative sense, of either the morbid affection for a deregulated liberty, or a system in which this affection seeks to justify itself. Let us strive to expose this affection, showing how it operates, and then define it.

It should be noted that this task is rendered all the more difficult, because Liberalism is already something vague, uncertain and indeterminable. It also extends to all domains: philosophy, theology, morality, law, economy, *etc.* and that, in all these domains it remains essentially variable according to the wiles of person and circumstance. This is why it is so difficult to pin it down, for it takes on many forms, including even the mask of truth and virtue.

Despite its varying characteristics, let us try to define it even if we do not succeed in reaching its full profundity. Hopefully we will at least be close to reality.

The True Notion of Liberty

Liberalism, as its name implies, presents itself as a system of liberty. But what is liberty? This again poses a problem, because this word also has a variety of meanings. In general, the word "liberty" suggests an idea of non-necessity, or the freedom from constraint. It signifies a certain independence and self-mastery. Without going into endless distinctions, let us note three principal meanings of liberty:

1) The external, physical liberty: a liberty of action and spontaneity (*Libertas a coactione*), which signifies the exemption of any exterior physical necessity or constraint, an absence of obstacles to natural activity. This liberty is common to man, animals, and even to lower forms of being.

2) Internal physical liberty or, "free will": (*libertas a necessitate*), the liberty of choice that exempts from any internal necessity. Rooted in spirituality, it makes man responsible for his acts. This liberty is proper to the intellectual being and opposed to determinism.

3) Moral liberty: This is the interior physical liberty which is reasonably limited by its object and perfected in its exercise[2] by the law which proceeds from a legitimate authority. Law traces the limits of the free will, which it cannot exceed, but which it can and must follow. In this sense, liberty is synonymous with right, and is expressed in the plural as liberties, franchisements and rights.

Other liberties are simple emanations of these three types. Thus, civil liberty is the faculty to accomplish, without hindrance, all legitimate acts of the citizen in the city. Political liberty consists of a reasonable and proportional participation of citizens in the affairs of common interest, carrying a certain

---

[2] From the moment that: "true perfection of any being is to search and find its end," or that liberty is; "the faculty to chose the means which will lead to a predetermined end" (free will), the law being an authentic order of means to an end, we conclude that liberty finds its perfection in its submission to the law and becomes "the faculty of self movement in good" (moral liberty). In God this is perfect since it identifies itself with the eternal law.

autonomy resulting in local and professional franchisements as much as circumstances require. These simple given facts will help to explain the Catholic concept of liberty compared to liberal concepts, and show by consequence, how much they differ and oppose each other.

The Catholic affirms and maintains to two principles: The reality of the free will of man contrary to any determinism, and, its necessary dependence upon God, His law, and all authority that proceeds from Him. Man is physically free, because he is gifted with a spiritual soul that is not determined by matter, nor is he obliged or morally necessitated, because of his dependence upon God and His laws. Coming from God, he freely returns to God, with the obligation however of conforming to His prescriptions. He must freely obey the moral necessity, his duty and God's law. As logical thought, ordaining its ideas according to their respective values, will guide the mind which submits itself to the law or to a scientific truth, so also will morality, ordaining its goods according to their values, render good to the free will. These in turn will guide him to the possession of his end, towards the perfecting of man. This is what we call the rational usage of the free will; limiting and guiding it to its end by the perfecting action of the law. In this way man, who is essentially free by nature, but none the less essentially dependent by his very condition, has the right or moral liberty to do only a part of that which he can. Consequently, to pool together all the elements of true liberty, we could say that it consists in this truly human activity, which is already freed by its very nature from the shackles of matter, (free will), governed and ordained in its choosing by God's law (moral liberty) and, also not hindered, but aided in its fundamental pursuit for its last end (liberty of action). Finally when the day comes that grace, which is the principle of the supernatural life, is added to this natural activity, we have that which we call Christian liberty. The whole law of this liberty is Charity, the intimate union with the infinite upright will of God. This Charity is in turn governed by the speculative and practical truth that submits man to God and delivers him from all that is unworthy of him. We owe all our respect to Christian liberty since it is the action of the Holy Ghost in man. This notion of true liberty helps us to understand that man must never be prevented from accomplishing those acts which God's law permits and prescribes. Pope Leo XIII described it splendidly by saying: "The faculty that enables him to operate in good; the faculty by which he may attain his end without hindrance."

The Liberal, on the contrary, turns these notions ambiguously upside-down, and from here, constructs an absolute right for his desires, wishes and caprices. He really cares little about free will, even becoming a partisan of determinism. When however he does so, he does it to accentuate his moral liberty and to free himself of all authority and responsibility. This causes in him a perfect confusion of liberty and independence, if of course this confusion had not been already there from the start. The Catholic proclaims that the free will is not something arbitrary, because the rational appetite must act according to reason, be regulated by authority and law, and finally ordain man to his last end. The Liberal makes of his liberty an end in itself.[3] His liberty becomes his law since it is sovereignly independent and autonomous. Catholic liberty becomes divine in its submission to God, while liberal liberty is self-destructive because it makes itself a god.

Let us look at an example to make this clearer: Both the Liberal and the Catholic preach "liberty of conscience." The Catholic however means to say that everyone has the faculty to know, love and serve God without being hindered. "The right to practice his religion and to see to it that the law of his country protect and support this" (Cardinal Andrieu), and thus the right of the Church to accomplish its mission in the world...*ut destructis adversitatibus et erroribus universis, Ecclesia tua secura tibi serviat libertate.*[4]

---

[3] Both beginning and end of authority: This is the liberty principle.
[4] The only true liberty of conscience, according to Pope Leo XIII (*Libertas*), the only one to defend as an inviolable right, consists of accomplishing one's duties to God and detesting, even if it should cost one's life, any order opposed to this sacred franchisement.

The Liberal wishes to affirm complete independence for every man from any religious belief, giving full reign to a belief in anything, or for that matter, to believe in nothing at all. This simply postulates the right of error and apostasy, and even the erection of laws in his country that would support him in his skepticism and disbelief.

So beware then. Let us not believe that when Pope Leo XIII speaks of liberty of conscience, and when a liberal speaks of the same, that they are talking about the same thing. Though the wording might be the same, the two meanings are totally opposed.

As Catholic liberty is a force regulated by faith and reason, channeled by law and authority, so the liberty of the liberal becomes synonymous to a variation of total independence from any rule, authority or law. Contrary to an ordered liberty, it becomes an anarchical liberty of the first degree. An analysis of facts and an enumeration of divers aspects of this Liberalism will help us to understand more clearly.

Aspects of Liberalism. Its Definition

The liberal is a fanatic for independence, and proclaims it in every domain, even unto absurdity:

- Independence of being from goodness and truth: this is the relative philosophy of "movement" and "becoming." A thing is no longer good and true in its being, it is now what it was not a moment ago, or vice versa.
- Independence of the intelligence from its object, *i.e.,* from the thing it is considering. Reason, which is now sovereign, no longer needs to submit itself to its object (any exterior reality). Reason is above truth, in fact, she creates her own! From here we have a radical evolution of truth; relative subjectivism.
- Independence of the will from the intelligence: an arbitrary and blind force; the will no longer looks upon the reason for judgment and estimation, but creates its own good just as the reason created its own truth.

- Independence of the conscience from an objective rule of law; she constitutes herself as supreme judge of morality.
- Independence of the anarchical powers of the sentiment from the reason: this is one of the characteristics of Romanticism, enemy of the preeminence of reason. From here man is guided according to his own sentiments. He claims a right to any movement of the passions. The result is immorality in its highest degree. (cf. Rousseau, Michelet...)
- Independence of the body from the soul; an unreasonable bestiality: this is the radical overturning of human values.
- Independence of the present from the historical past; from whence the scorn for tradition and the morbid love of novelties under the pretext of progress.
- Independence of reason and science from the faith: this is rationalism by which the reason becomes the sovereign judge and measure of truth, considers herself self-sufficient, and rejects any exterior domination.
- Independence of the individual from society; of the child from his parents, of the wife from her husband, of the citizen from the State, of the faithful from the Church. This is the anarchical individualism, by which man, who is naturally good (Rousseau) or in fatal progress (Payot, Bayet) can evolve in his own manner, in total liberty and in living his own self-centered life. Any attack on this sacred liberty is tyrannical, despotic and a crime of high treason against humanity.
- Independence of the worker from his employer; from whence the tendency to substitute a cooperative hierarchy with a cooperative equality, and, by participation in benefices and profit, and by the share holding worker, a march towards industrial Sovietism.
- Independence of man, the family, man's profession, and, above all, of the State from God, Jesus Christ and the Church. This is, accordingly, naturalism, secular-

ism, latitudinarism, and has as consequence, the "modern liberties," venerated as divinities of the future.
- Independence of the people and their representatives from God. Popular sovereignty and universal vote as the measure of truth and goodness, and source of every right in a nation. From thence the official apostasy of the people rejecting the social reign of Our Lord Jesus Christ and their failure to recognize the divine authority of the Church.

These are a few of the principal aspects of Liberalism, chaos of errors, a truly uncontrolled monster. Like Protestantism, Kantianism, Secularism, and Modernism, it is the rendezvous of all heresies. What can we say about its universal influence? It contains all other heresies because it is their principle and source. This description helps us to understand its nature more profoundly and so brings us to its definition: It is above all the overturning of all values, a contradiction of law and order. In this general sense, we define Liberalism according to Rev. Fr. de Pascal: "In every walk of life, the deregulation of true liberty," or, more precisely, "the system that pretends to justify the practical disorientation of liberty by the theoretical overthrowing of values." True liberty, as we have said, is nothing other than "the faculty to choose the means, ordaining them to the end." Therefore, there is no legitimate liberty that is not ordained through the law which in turn determines the means and the end. If it is not within this framework, liberty becomes licentiousness. Liberalism is precisely the negation of order, law and authority.

But Liberalism is far from being a coherent doctrine or a formulated system. It is rather a sickness of the mind, an orientation rather than a school, a perversion of sentiment based on pride, or a state of mind rather than a sect. Liberalism appears then as "a disordered affection of man for his independent liberty, which makes him abhor any limit, bond, yoke or discipline from the law or from authority." It is a radical perversity opposed to wisdom and is the caricature of order. Wisdom sees everything in its correct perspective because it considers it from the most elevated outlook, even from God's perspective, and so reveres all order. Liberalism, on the contrary, sees everything from the perspective of man, and most often even from the less noble side of man, deriving everything from this defective view. The result is the corruption of his intelligence and affections, and finally the disorder in his actions. In this measure, Liberalism is a passion, a fanaticism, a religion...an incurable sickness.

Such then is the general understanding of Liberalism, either as a system or as a state of mind. We can now more easily proceed to follow its history, formulate its synthesis, and after having unmasked it, go on to indicate appropriate remedies.

Chapter I

ORIGINS OF LIBERALISM, HISTORICAL DEVELOPMENTS, ACTUAL STATE OF AFFAIRS

First Origin

The term, "Liberalism" is rather recent. It seems to have come from a Mme. de Stael, but the thing itself, on the contrary, is as old as the hills. The father of Liberalism is naturally he who first revolted, Satan himself.

Proudly refusing the supernatural and necessary gift of grace so as not to depend further on his Author and Benefactor, claiming to attain to it by his own strength, and complacently considering the excellence of his own splendid nature he launched in the heights of heaven the first cry of rebellion, *non serviam, I shall not serve.*

At this cry of disobedience, St. Michael victoriously overcame him with the affirmation of the supreme right of God: *Quis ut Deus, who is like unto God!* Thus St. Michael became the model and patron of all who would defend of the rights of God.[1]

Man had hardly been created, when Satan incited him to disobey God. Consequently, man found himself limited in his exercise of liberty. This was the first sin, original sin, source of

---

[1] Pope Leo XIII also accuses Satan as the originator of Liberalism: "But there are very many who, following the example of Lucifer from whom comes the name criminal, cry with him *non serviam* and take 'liberty' as nothing other than pure licentiousness. Such are those belonging to that school, so spread out and powerful, who would like to borrow their name from liberty, and so wish to be called 'Liberals'" (Pope Leo XIII, *Libertas Praestantissimum*—Available from Angelus Press).

radical disorder. Because of his revolt against God, Adam would find his lower faculties at war within himself. Having rejected the noble service of God, man became a miserable slave of creation and of his own passions. From now on, fallen nature experienced an overturning of all its values, and, a continual battle of tendencies growing under the commission of personal sins. It could no longer find within itself that objective moral law of human activity. In order for it to find correction, it was obliged to turn to the immutable, pure and Eternal Law, to the natural law or to the positive law derived from these. We see today how, those who teach that nature should simply be followed,[2] begin by denying the existence of original sin, or, perverting the teaching thereof, claim that nature is essentially good and destined to inevitable change. They go so far as to divinize it in the past or in the future, and in the present to place no obstacle to it. In this way they lay down the premise of a proud disorder. Man, doubly miserable as creature and sinner, promoted as an equal with God, becomes his own law, absolutely free to think and do as he pleases. This is what we may call an "immanent life."

Protestantism—Luther

Liberalism therefore always existed, and even if we call it "Modern ideas or aspirations," it still dates from Satan and original sin. It is nevertheless, from the time of Luther, in the 16th century, that Liberalism began to be imposed as a system and doctrinal formula.

Shaking off the teaching authority of the Church, this rebellious monk, Luther, proclaimed individual liberty as a principle in the religious domain. But in the very process of proclaiming this "free thinking," he also "opened," as Pope Leo XIII said, "the

---

[2] "Naturalists...deny that the father of the human race sinned, and by consequence, reject the fact that the operations of free will are defective and inclined to evil. On the contrary, they exaggerate the powers and excellence of nature, attributing to it only the principles and rules of Justice. They cannot even conceive the necessity of making constant efforts and courageous acts in order to suppress nature and impose silence upon the appetites" (Pope Leo XIII, *Humanum Genus*).

way to infinite variations, doubts and negations concerning even the most important matters." The logic of these ideas is more powerful than the intention of those who issued them. Luther completely disregarded the authority of supernatural truths, falsified the notions of original sin and Justification, and rejected the hierarchy and rights of authority in the Church. The audacity of his principle of free thinking, extended its devastation into every domain of philosophy with Descartes and Kant, of social and political thought with Rousseau and Tolstoy, and even of "orthodox" Protestantism itself. This last was brought about in stages, through the necessary step of liberal protestantism, and quickly became a mass of naturalistic and rationalistic doctrines (unless one rejects its principle, but then the path is immediately traced back to Catholicism).

Naturalism and Rationalism

From the time of pagan Renaissance[3] and the Protestant revolution, there is a progressive development of naturalism and rationalism in thought, institutions and law.

Notion and Definition

Naturalism is the system that seeks systematically to eliminate God and His supreme sovereignty over the order of things in the world called "nature." It rejects God from public life in the name of liberty of conscience, which will later become "secularism." Next, it throws out every aspect of the supernatural, even in private life. The Providential God still bothers the secularist, and so, on step further on, we arrive at some vague deism. Finally, God disappears completely, or, even becomes one with man, the state or the world. Thus "nature" is liberated and Naturalism has arrived at its final aim.

Rationalism differs little from Naturalism, but presents itself more explicitly as a system of knowledge where the autonomous reason of man becomes the supreme and only arbiter of truth and

---

[3] "Since the Renaissance, the multitude has striven to grasp an excessive degree of liberty" (Pope Leo XIII, *Diuturnum*).

error, of good and evil.[4] This is why, following the example of Pope Pius IX's *Syllabus*, we do not separate them.

The "Separated" Philosophy: Descartes, Kant, Cousin

Disorder always begins in the intellect, even before it is formulated into a system, and influenced by personal interests or passion. Let us first explain.

The human philosophy of Aristotle and the Christian philosophy of the Fathers of the Church conforms both to common sense and to the development of Catholic dogma which is so well expounded in Thomistic synthesis. That which was for so long a time its nobility and power, was its submission, by a glorious service, to Sacred Doctrine, and in this it showed itself once again faithful to its own principles.

This fruitful union was broken by Descartes, the father of "modern" or "separated" philosophy. Proudly separating himself from true scholastic tradition, Descartes wished to build his own philosophical edifice. He was able to spread the germs of his most contradictive errors: idealism, materialism, empiricism and subjectivism. This is already the liberal in his pure essence. The intelligence is no longer held to humbly submit to reality; it is independent of things, waiting to create them, and to form them according to its own desire and measure. Many elements have already faded away in the works of Descartes; we have kept only the worst. From this Cartesian revolution, wrote Mr. Penjon, the modern thought has kept only, and more precisely, the spirit of free research that makes the individual reason, judge of truth and error.

Kant had only to draw his conclusions: the autonomy and the perfect immanence of the human intelligence. Of his own criticisms, his artificial and complicated system, many details have also disappeared. Again, the only thing that remains is that perfidious venom injected by Descartes: the independence of the

---

[4] "The principle of Rationalism, is the sovereign dominion of the human reason, which refuses obedience to the divine and eternal reason. It considers only itself as self-sufficient, supreme principle and source and judge of truth" (Pope Leo XIII, *Libertas*).

intelligence in regard to its object and in regard to the Faith. Hence, the essential relativity of truth and its radical evolution in man, with man, and by man. This is also the foundation of rationalism which makes the human reason and its ideological contents the measure of what is.[5]

Cousin will continue with Descartes and will adapt Kant to fit in with French thought. Even the name of his system, eclecticism, manifests his principle. The reason, sovereign legislator of truth, will choose truth, beauty and goodness in all independence and measure according to its own taste.

"Philosophism": Bayle, Diderot, Voltaire

Also, upon a less speculative plane, is born the development of "philosophism"[6] (18th Century). Flowing forth logically from Protestantism, Locke, Hume and other philosophers professed that only truths which the reason can attain and prove, can exist. They willingly present themselves under the trait of an amicable skepticism, but in reality, are fanatical adorers of nature and reason. They preach universal tolerance, but under the condition that it supports error only, because they manifest a violent hatred against Our Lord Jesus Christ, His Church and everything supernatural.

In the beginning of this century we have Bayle, who was of Calvinistic origin. His system is one of skepticism, by which he announces that since truth is inaccessible, no one can boast to possess it and therefore no one has the right to impose it upon others. Though a skeptic, he has nevertheless a vigorous confidence in reason when it concerns attacking the Church and Her dogmas.

The *Encyclopaedia* (Diderot and D'Alembert), apparently a synthesis of human knowledge, was in reality a war machine that

---

[5] Maritain, *Trois Reformateurs—The Three Reformers*, p.122.

[6] "The 'philosophes' of the last century largely contributed to the evil wave (of Liberalism) upon France, when, infatuated with a false wisdom, they began to overturn the foundations of Christian truths and invented their own system in order to develop an ardent love for liberty without limits" (Pope Leo XIII, *Nobilissima Gallorum Gens*).

continued the work of the dictionary of Bayle against the supernatural. In these we find the principle ideas which will soon be used to systematize the Liberalism of the 19th century: "suppression of every absolute, of every miracle, of every mystery, of all metaphysics, of every constraint, liberty of thought, of speech, acting and living, universal tolerance" with the exception of anything that would show the least favor to the intolerant Roman Church (Fr. Calvet).

But the greatest of all intellectual malefactors of this century of decadence and corruption in the religious domain, is without doubt, the infamous Voltaire. Although being a believer in a vague and somewhat irritating deism, he began to attack with a Satanic rage Jesus Christ and His Church. He truly became the king of this century, *et siluit terra in conspectu ejus...et exaltatum est et elevatum cor ejus*; but a horrible end awaited him, *et post haec decidit in lectum et cognovit quia moreretur*.[7] The Church buried him like all others and immortally continues Her work of redemption and salvation.

Revolutionary Philosophy: Rousseau, the Revolution

The principles of Naturalism and Rationalism have not yet stopped producing their consequences. Grace, it is true, preserves nature while it also perfects her, but from the moment that nature rejects the salutary yoke of Jesus Christ and the Magisterium of His Church, the disoriented reason is no longer capable of safeguarding natural notions, which are at the very base of political and social order.

Here again, Protestantism opens the way with the pastor Jurieu, (17th century) and the Genevan Rousseau, the "saint of nature" as Jacques Maritain calls him. The influence of this eloquent sophist has penetrated all of contemporary society and the modern world so profoundly with these institutions and laws, that even those who today attack him, are affected by his philosophy. According to Rousseau, man is originally and essentially

---

[7] "And the earth was quiet before him. His heart was exalted and lifted up....And after these things, he fell down upon his bed and knew that he should die" (I Macc. 1:3-6).

good by nature; from this principle results the negation of original sin and redemption, the rejection of any link, limitation, or authority that would seek to stop and regulate such a nature. Everything that this nature may think of, may say, or might wish to do, can only be good. This, by way of consequence, is a radical dissolution of society whether religious, domestic or political. In this last domain, Rousseau logically derives an egalitarian democracy where every individual may freely obey because every individual equally commands. This causes a perpetual oscillation between the oppressive centralization of the omnipotent State and the anarchical, no less tyrannical, unbridled demagogy.

The "Societies of thought," the Masonic lodges, were the factories where the formulas of this naturalistic and rationalistic cult were produced. These were the seminaries that produced these fanatical and sectarian apostles. Thanks to their activity, the reformist movement of 1789 rapidly became revolutionary. This was the universal triumph of Rationalism. D. Benoit correctly defined this revolution according to its profound characteristics as the "organized revolt against the public right of the Church and therefore against the social reign of Our Lord Jesus Christ." "The revolution," he wrote, "is the changing of the ancient political and social order that was deeply penetrated with Christian influence and founded upon the Gospel." Though this order underwent certain alterations, it kept the powerful imprint of religion. The revolution, on the contrary, established a new order (if we can so call it) founded upon reason only. Recently, the revolution was honored for its restoration of civil and political equality, conforming these to the pure spirit of the Gospel. In reality, the revolution, under the pretext of equality, suppressed all useful privileges, and entitled organizations by substituting hierarchical liberties with a foolish and most dangerous independence. Considering it from a correct perspective, the revolution appears above all as a practical bringing into effect of "philosophism," that is, an essentially anti-Catholic Rationalism. De Bonald defined it as "a call upon every passion by means of every error."

Romanticism: Mme. de Stael, Chateaubriand, Michelet, Victor Hugo

A "scourge," would perhaps have been a better word for Romanticism. Romanticism is disorder and, excluding perhaps a few appearances, it was, and still is, the propagator of disorder. Rejecting the presidency of the reason, it gives itself to caprices of obscure sentiments, to wild imaginations and instincts, in short, to all that is common with animals. It paradoxically cares for the individual, for the cult of the *"ego"* and passions. In its instinctive and violent operation, it throws itself in ridiculous veneration at the feet of the sacred liberty of the individual. It seeks to glorify the irregular, the crazy, the criminal, and finishes with the exaltation of the perverse individual, tempting even to rehabilitate Satan himself. It has also profound affinities with the Revolution, which it admires with emphasis: Before 1789, it was force, servitude, superstition, every power of evil, but, with the Revolution, it's the reign of Right, Justice, Liberty, and Reason. Perhaps this explanation is seen to be simplistic, but these things nevertheless form the foundation of its rudimentary philosophy of history. Let us add to this the ridiculous hatred for the past and the idolatry of the future as a religion of progress, of an undefined progress, fatal, sublime, and ending through science and democracy to an unscathed Justice, to a heavenly brotherhood.

Such is Romanticism[8] that has formed, molded and fashioned the minds of the 19th century. It proceeds from Rousseau, Mme. de Stael, Chateaubriand and blossoms with Michelet and Victor Hugo. It is found authentically in the mentality of the great leaders and modern "theologians" of democracy, and of secularism, and deeply imprints its indelible mark on the best products of the official school.

Modern Liberalism: Tolstoy, Jaurès, Buisson

Modern Liberalism, heir of all preceding errors, is nothing other than a new name for ancient Naturalism and Rationalism. It accentuates not nature, reason or science, but above all, liberty.

---

[8] P. Lasserre also defined it as: "a partaking of absolute individualism in thought and sentiment."

The Liberalism of the 19th century manifests an anarchical and deregulated liberty in every domain. Absolute autonomy of the individual, of his reason and will, the liberty of thought, of conscience and undefined progress even unto the deification of man. Thus, it always remains faithful to its name, motto, and banner; liberty by principle, autonomous and independent. Whether we consider Tolstoy, the Rousseau of Russia, or Jaurès, the loud voice of international socialism in France, we have the same efficacious agent of dechristianization and social decomposition.

Today, thanks to Freemasonry, to the government that it controls, and to the school that it directs, the great natural and supernatural truths are obscured, and Liberalism triumphs ever more among the masses under the name of "secularism." Many of its proselytes are, ironically, of Jewish descent. They hold in government, administration, the courts and the universities, the most influential and important posts. In this category of "intellectual malefactors," the most representative type would be F. Buisson, grand master of the lay school of thought.

I say "grand master" because Liberalism, today termed secularism, appears more and more to have the characteristics of a philosophy, a sect or a religion. It is a "secular faith," an "affirmation of the modern conscience" opposed to the rights of God and the Church. Always, it remains the spirit of Luther, of Descartes, Rousseau, Kant, Hegel, which constitutes its invariable foundation and ends with exactly the same consequences. Certainly, it slowly abandons Rousseau's fable of the original bounty of man. But, following the theories of the evolutionists, it turns towards the fatal, necessary, undefinable progress of the deification of man and humanity from a grotesque animality or even from that primitive cloud of matter.

Obscure idealism, bilious democracy, revolutionary mysticism....All this is plainly ridiculous and absurd. It merits only disdain from any healthy and realistic mind. Sadly, we are obliged to say, we loose all desire to laugh when we see most of our official teachers hard at work inculcating these most dangerous dogmas into the hearts of the immense majority of the children of France.*

---

    *   [Translator's Note] These things were said and written of France in 1926. *Post factum*, it is now not only easy to see; it has become obvious and this for the entire world. From the moment the Church opened wide her doors to the modern world at the Second Vatican Council, she swallowed in all these pernicious philosophies.

Chapter II

LOGICAL DEVELOPMENT AND SYNTHESIS OF LIBERALISM

As we have said, Liberalism is a recent name for the old heresies of Protestantism, Naturalism and Rationalism....Though the label is different, the principles remain the same and the results bad. If the substance however remains, the point of view changes, which justifies the use of different names.

Liberalism considers liberty in everything, in every domain and from every point of view. From the independence and autonomy of man, it continues to seek and reorganize everything according to this new dogma. In the name of "liberty of conscience," Liberalism rejects every supremacy of spiritual authority over temporal authority. It also rejects any exterior religious authority over the individual conscience, and supplies its principle to updated "secularism."

When Liberalism seeks to construct some system for its teachings, it acknowledges that its essential dogmas, as axiom or postulation of principle, are: "Liberty, complete autonomy, absolute independence, exemption from any law that does not proceed from the individual, or is not agreed upon by him, and the suppression of any fetter which might bother him." Thus he is a liberal in philosophy, a liberal in morals and sociology, and a free thinker in religion.

Let us systematically follow its diverse manifestations, first in pure philosophy, then in morality and religion, and finally, by means of a special study, in politics.

In General Philosophy

Modern Liberalism seeks to first attack the fundamental order of the metaphysics of knowledge. It mistrusts intellectualism, and that, perhaps with a grain of truth. It especially attacks Thomistic philosophy as being too submitted to its object, too servile with regards to dogma, and imposing, on the other hand, an insupportable constraint upon the appetitive and affective powers. Consequently, by means of a certain philosophical romanticism, it seeks to find any system that would assure more liberty; Subjective idealism (Kant), Objective idealism (Fichte), voluntarism, moralism, pragmatism, philosophy of action or intuition, even the unbridled liberalisms of Renouvier, Secretan or Lequier. According to these last mentioned, everything is subordinate to the free will, which in turn depends upon nothing else. God is no longer considered as He who is, but, He who wishes, *i.e.,* absolute liberty. Objective evidence, certitude, first principles, especially the question of contradictions, are unpardonable evils since they impose limits and painful constraints upon the free thinker. Of course, by this process we end up denying every law of logic and assume that every affirmation is free. For Descartes, judgment is not an assenting of the intelligence, but a consenting of the will! With people like Bergson and Le Roy, the conclusion is simply the radical evolution of truth. Truth no longer is, but rather, is made; essentially variable, freely formulated, freely accepted. Its existence and value depends solely upon the subject who adheres to it or is in accordance with it. From now on, it is the individual mind which creates all truth, reality included, and evidently, that includes God Himself.

This autonomous liberty of mind that is both sovereign and inviolable, is sacred. "Tying down the reason," wrote F. Buisson, "putting pressure upon the intellect, that is a sacrilege." Truth itself does not have the right to enslave the intelligence. If it was uniform and definite, it would indeed tie her down. Simply put, there are no truths, no absolute certitudes. Intolerant affirmations are no longer to be sustained; only generous and large impressions. The mind is no longer submitted to the constrained and tyrannical domination of truth. "It is its own norm, a moving and susceptible norm which changes indefinitely according to the wiles of the individual sense." This is universal relativism. If each and everyone follows the light coming from his subconscience only, then *a fortiori*, he does not have the right to accept a doctrine affirmed by another, even if this other is God Himself. Truth comes from the interior, following an immanent and vital drive from the profound sentiment of the individual. This will go so far as to prefer the error freely found to the truth servilely received. Thus the "Free Thinker" is necessarily led to the "Free thought." Why then waste your time thinking?

The only truth therefore is that there is no absolute truth. The mind is inviolably free regarding all truth. It is free especially from that which would seek to do violence in the name of an exterior authority, as for example, the revealed truth.

It is no longer difficult to understand that a person like Jaurès, disciple of Hegel, before he became one of Karl Marx, was able to write:

> What we have to safeguard above all...through all prejudices, sufferings and battles, is the inestimable good of man which is the idea that there is no sacred truth. There is nothing prohibited for man to totally investigate. The sovereign liberty of the mind is the greatest thing in the world. Every truth that does not come from us is a lie. Even every adhesion that we give, should go hand in hand with our critical sense that always watches, and produces a secret revolt. This must always be admixed with every affirmation and thought. Even if the idea of God be made visible, if God Himself should appear before us palpably, the first duty of man would be to refuse obedience and consider Him as an equal with whom he can argue and not as a master to whom he submits.

Logically then we can only conclude the principle of Rationalism; the individual reason, judge of truth and error, of good and evil, source of all reality, the creator of God Himself.

In Religion and Morality

Of course there is no question of supernatural religion or morality for the liberal. A truth or commandment that seeks to impose itself upon man from the exterior is for the liberal unassimilable and totally unintelligible. It would be an immoral violence and sacrilege, an insupportable attack upon the sacrosanct liberty of the individual.

But even the notions of natural religion and morality are corrupted and suppressed by the radical destruction of their foundations which are the metaphysical truths of God and man.

What is God for the liberal? He is either nothing, and this would be radical atheism; or He is everything and this would be Pantheism; or He is only a something but not a person and this would be the making of an idol. God is then reduced to a simple ideal representation which the human mind, by accommodation, would make respectable. The Liberal would rather speak about the "divine" than about "God." This divine already well enfeebled, would remain a "notion perpetually revisable" submitted to any limitations that the sovereign reason of man could arbitrarily impose. It is Reason, who created "him" (or it) in conceptions and expressions. Of course, we are on the door step of Modernism, but then again, Liberalism is in fact its very foundation.

Man is free, essentially free, absolutely free. Yet the Liberal recognizes one fundamental obligation only: to respect, conserve and foster this unlimited liberty. Please, no longer mention any authority, bond or law. This would be servitude, and "servitude," wrote F. Buisson, "is a crime of high treason against humanity, without even excepting that servitude which is believed to be voluntary." The unique rule of morality is the free act, and such only, is a good act. Respect the liberty of others! That is the entire law of morality. "Charity" (with the foundation of faith) "is the entire law;" says St. Paul. "Liberty sums up morality," replies the liberal. Once again the total emancipation of the individual is nothing other than his deification. However, for the more recent fabricators of liberal "morality," this substitution of God by man can only take place progressively, thanks to democratic institutions and legislation which is becoming ever more secularized. Such is the irreligion of tomorrow or the liberty of conscience that will soon find itself blossoming in its acquisition of the attributes of God Himself. Thought is liberated from truth and dogmas of faith. The individual (or social) conscience, supreme norm of good, finds in itself the laws of its own activity, the dignity of man, liberty, an end in itself, absolute autonomy of the will; these are the principles of the new morality. We have always believed, on the contrary, that liberty was submitted to order. For the liberal, order consists in the respect of liberty, supreme cause and last end of itself.

A sober and sane mind is stupefied in the presence of such ridiculous and monstrous aberrations. And yet, these are the teachings injected into our schools, and forced upon our children. Man is promoted to God, or at least he is soon to become a god in virtue of necessary progress. Science will bring man, his conscience and reason through this immanent life, so content in itself, to the point of "divinity." For the behind-the-times disciples of Rousseau, it is nature that is all good; for others it is nature which is all evil; but for one and all, it is liberty that is the ideal because she will be the final blossoming of nature, or the final conqueror of it all. She will be the victorious goodness itself. Religion and the morality of man trying to become God are altogether summed up in a liberty without limits and without any brakes. Payot wrote:

> Human progress is obliged to bring forth liberty more and more. Man must successively overcome the oppression of nature, the hereditary violence from ancestry, milieu and traditions. He is politically free...indeed proud and free,...conscious of his value and dignity, who wants to obey the laws of his own reason only.[1]

These laws, however, are according to him extremely simple. Thus, this author continues a few pages further: "Truth is not...it is made." This follows an evolution, which, if it is not opposed, will rapidly bring man to the summit of divinity.

It is terrible to see theories so absurd. We must certainly be indignant to see these teachings proposed and imposed upon our unfortunate children, baptized and redeemed by the blood of God.

By their universal application and profound influence, these philosophical, moral and religious doctrines, essentially produce a state of mind that gives an orientation to the activity of man. We will later extricate the consequences produced in practice by the dissolving principles of Liberalism. Nevertheless, it does not take

---

[1] *Cours de Morale*, p.104.

much to surmise the ruin that this unbridled individualism will produce in social, political and economic domains: The family is destroyed, marriage reduced to a simple revisable contract (divorce and free union), and the authority of the husband and father trampled down (emancipation of woman and children). Civil society becomes purely conventional while authority is weakened and destroyed. The people are sovereign, which turns out to be a deceptive sovereignty since regimes born from revolutionary philosophy strive to suppress liberty in the name of liberty itself. Economically speaking, corporations which guaranteed and safeguarded the rights of both employees and employers, assuring thereby social peace and order, are being suppressed. Tomorrow it will be State Collectivism, revolutionary Syndicalism or pure Communism.

Chapter III

POLITICAL AND SOCIAL LIBERALISM

As we have already said, Liberalism adopts many different forms according to persons, circumstances and the general area upon which it evolves. Up to now, we have considered it in a profound philosophical sense, so as to better understand the various practical applications. It is impossible to study all its possible applications, but there is one application in particular, because of its intrinsic importance, to which we must give our special attention: this is Political and Social Liberalism.

It is, we should add, to this particular form that many modern authors really attribute the designation of "Liberalism." People like Cardinal Pie, Canon Perin, Pope Leo XIII[1] and Cardinal Billot consider Liberalism as the application of the principles of Naturalism and Rationalism to Social and Political order, especially regarding the Church and State. Accordingly they explain Liberalism as "the more or less accentuated emancipation of the State from the Church," or, "the negation of the supernatural order applied in Politics," or, "a political-religious system that implicitly or explicitly denies the divine authority of the Church, proclaiming the supremacy of the State above the Church, or the autonomy and independence of the State in its relations to the Church."

We have seen that the fundamental principle of Liberalism is the concept of an independent liberty from all authority, law or

---

[1] "What the partisans of Naturalism and Rationalism are in philosophy, the scoundrels of Liberalism are in the moral and civil order, since they introduce in morality as well as in daily life the principles held by the partisans of Naturalism" (Pope Leo XIII, *Libertas*).

bond, which is the supreme good of man. It is the corner stone of the edifice, the norm of all appreciation and activity, the unique source of rights and duties...

Let us now follow its principle in the application to the political-religious order and see for ourselves the mess it leaves behind.

Civil Society—The State according to Liberalism

The central dogma remains the absolute autonomy of the individual, the essential liberty of man.

If by chance or be it by necessity man enters society, he is in no way required to abdicate his dignity nor his sacrosanct liberty. Upon entering society, he nevertheless remains free to leave and if however he wishes to remain, it would be under the condition that he remains completely free. The requirement would be that he has no superior, force or external law to obey; thus full liberty postulates an absolute equality regarding his associates.

It then follows that no authority of force or riches could exist in such a conventional association: this is the common-anarchist tendency. Authority might be allowed only as far as it plays the role of respecting and making respect the absolute liberty of man: this is the liberalist-individual and the anti-State of Montesquieu. Finally the social organization is the most apt to safeguard the liberty of the individual and consists in making kings of all citizens and erecting a sovereign people: this is the violently centralized and Statist tendency of J. J. Rousseau.

According to the conception of Rousseau, Society or the State, constituted by an arbitrary contract of free and equal individuals, simply becomes the ensemble of all these same individuals. These become a sovereign people who absorb all power. Soon this will become the State-God of Hegel. The State is therefore the highest power, supreme authority and finality of the progress of man. There is nothing above it, and it has the final say. All authority comes from the State that precedes every law and right. If the people choose representatives for the execution of certain affairs, the State loses none of its inalienable sovereignty. Whatever the adopted system or constitution may be, man, or the citizen, really only obeys himself, even if he is not always aware of it.

But what happens to the Church in such a system? She becomes a simple association which owes her very existence to the State, even receiving all her rights from it. This association will be considered as rebellious if she by chance should consider herself autonomous; she will even become immoral if she should try to impose upon the individual or collective conscience any obligation that would put their liberty in danger.

These are but logical consequences flowing from the "liberty of conscience" imposed by Liberalism as an absolute right and law in itself. Liberty of conscience, as we have already shown, is the absolute power of the individual to believe or not to believe, within the limits of the civil law. This liberty becomes the guarantee of all liberties and is even the very source of justice. No one can claim to possess the truth exclusively. Every one is obliged to practice a universal tolerance of respect for the conscience and beliefs of others. The only ones excluded from this generous tolerance would be those professing doctrines, or, those in religious sects who seek to impose their truth or cult and exclude all others. The Roman Pantheon gives a perfect image of this, since it offered hospitality to all divinities except to the Christian God who is too unsociable as to support the others.

The dogma of liberty of conscience has as necessary corollary the absolute secularism of the State. If every one can think and believe as he wishes, and if the State is nothing other than an arithmetical sum of individuals, then it follows that the State cannot impose any belief, neither favor one at the cost of another, nor even consider any...only if necessary to assure peace and order among individuals or between religions. This will inevitably cause the taking sides against those religions or sects, which by their fanatical and sacrilegious intolerance, would dare to infringe upon the liberty of other beliefs or religions. Thus the radical negation of a religion of the State leads invariably to an irreligion of the State and finally to persecution.

Universal Secularism

Catholics have always seen, in the secularism of the State, and all organisms that would depend upon it, an evil intention to make war upon the Church, to suppress the Catholic conscience and violate her liberty. Rash and bitter Judgment some say. The liberty of conscience preached and proclaimed by all is only a methodical and prudent application of secularism. The Catholic Church was not aimed at more than the Protestants or even the Jewish Synagogue! If only she herself would recognize liberty of conscience; if only she would accept the supremacy of the State, then in exchange for this, tolerance and even benevolence would be given to her.

There is, they say, no need to remind the State of its solemn promise to assure liberty of conscience to all, since, do not forget, that is its essential duty, and precisely because it wishes to accomplish this task, it has devoted itself with a praiseworthy courage to fulfill this work of emancipation, called universal secularization:

- Firstly, secularization of the State itself: Religious questions are the affairs of the private conscience. The majestic State, situated way above and beyond religious affairs, is totally indifferent. She seeks to protect them all, and under no circumstances will she be a disciple of any. Thus, Churches and religions are in the State and receive from it their very existence and the law of their activity. Those then who refuse to submit to the civil law, which is the expression of the general will, and seek to limit themselves to strict common justice, are not worthy of the benevolent tolerance of the State. Thus secularization of the State is the same as the separation of Church and State, and has as consequence the legal persecution of the Catholic Church.
- Secularization of legislation, administration and politics: These simply remain rigorous consequences of the supremacy of reason and sovereignty of the people. In virtue of the liberty of conscience, the code of law will be purged of any trace of religion. Administration will only accept lay people who are in accordance with its own mind and judgment. Of course, national and international politics will no longer take account of God, Jesus Christ, the Church, the Pope or of Religion. "The gov-

ernment of the affairs of this world must pass from the evangelical doctors to the disciples of reason."
- Secularization of education: Again in virtue of the liberty of conscience, the school must withdraw itself from the hold of churches, especially the Catholic Church. It must escape her authority and her direction so that it may be remitted exclusively into the hands of the State. The State alone is the yardstick, since it alone is neutral and gives a purely natural teaching without oppressing or offending any conscience. The State will be the only official educator and have complete monopoly. Her education will be free of charge so that even the poor may profit by it; it will also be obligatory so that no one can escape; it will be secular in its direction, personnel, doctrines and programs, that is, essentially rationalistic, so that all opinions may be respected. Soon it will be unique so as not to have two distinct and rival groups of youth; all minds will express the same liberty of conscience and finally taste the peace and happiness in a wide and universal tolerance.
- In a parallel way, the State will produce, little by little the secularization of justice, marriage, funerals, the army, navy, centers of charity, hospitals....So, man will be free in a free State.

The War against the Catholic Hierarchy

To believe in a revealed Religion, imposed by an exterior authority over human reason, is without doubt very humiliating for the liberal, and therefore, profoundly immoral. It is a crime of high treason and a sacrilege. Nevertheless, the secular and generous State, will not begin an Inquisition, even though she could do it since the liberation of consciences is enslaved by Catholicism.

The State will therefore, in the meantime, tolerate the Catholic belief of the individual who so loves his chain and collar. But the State cannot accept an ecclesiastical hierarchy which claims her independence. By consequence, respecting (or at least being tolerant) of the individual's Catholic Religion, it nevertheless has to combat the ecclesiastical hierarchy, this theocracy or "clericalism." It will first change religious orders and their vows, which are profoundly immoral and whose activity can cause many dangers. After this it will confiscate all goods from the secular clergy, suppressing any immunity on their part. This will make them simple public servants and later, they will be completely suppressed. Regarding Bishops, the State will closely survey their nomination and administration, and will try to submit the assembly of Bishops to their own faithful. Finally, to enslave the national Church, if it is not able to destroy her, the State will separate her from the authority of that "stranger," the Pope...

Such then is the Masonic plan of political and social Liberalism: an absolute liberty of conscience, secularization of the State, universal secularism of the nation, a war against the hierarchy and therefore against the Catholic Religion since the Church is part of this Catholic Creed. Everything follows smoothly and logically. Now for a few words regarding its historical development.

A Historical Sketch on Political and Social Liberalism

The State today is wholly impregnated with Liberalism and actively propagates it. Before being a faithful apostle, it has become a slave. It seems to believe that it has done more to assure the triumph of this system of "secular faith," than to be the humble organ of the common good.

It was however not always like this. Pope Leo XIII in his encyclical *Immortale Dei*, brings to memory with joy, the "times when the evangelical wisdom governed the empires," and Pope St. Pius X, in his encyclical against the Sillon, willingly brings to mind the great monarchs, who in accordance with the Church, gloriously governed nations. The 13th century of "Christendom" established the most beautiful triumph of "Christian justice." In that epoch, wrote Pope Leo XIII, the influence of Christian wisdom and her divine virtue penetrated laws and institutions, the morals of the people of every rank and position in civil society:

> Though everything was not perfect, nevertheless, we were on the right road towards a peace which would be obtained by the universal submission to the obligatory and bountiful social reign of Our Lord Jesus Christ. *Pax Christi in regno Christi.*

But with impatience did the civil power support the authority of the Church and the Roman Pontiff. The German emperors, Henry IV, Frederick Barbarossa and Frederick II, continued their long strife between the priesthood and the empire. These were accompanied by apparently humble personages who became their precious counselors. They were very active and had ambitious aims, these were what we called the Legalists. It is not hard to see how they became the most authentic ancestors of modern liberals.

These legalists, preoccupied with Roman and Byzantine laws, filled with memories of the Emperor Pontiffs, sought to exempt the State from the jurisdiction of the Church and even to subordinate the national churches to it. This would perfectly fall into place with their mania for the centralization and legal despotism.

In France they began to appear especially with Phillip the Fair. Thanks also to the Renaissance and Protestant revolution, their role and influence expanded at the cost of Catholic civilization. They would rather use the civil power to arrive at their own end, than to use it for the common good. They began to limit by means of a detrimental centralizing action, provincial autonomies, franchised corporations, individual liberties and all natural organisms which supported the common good. They used the civil power to enslave the Church, even unto the day that they would see in the Monarchy, though "very Christian," an obstacle to universal secularization. They did not hesitate to overthrow it (1789-1793) to install in its place the triumph of the legalists and the definitive era of the "new Justice." Historians such as Taine, P. de la Gorce, Gautherot and G. Bord, show that from that moment, the roles of lawyers, legalists, parliamentary councilors, justices of peace, magistrates *etc.* became preponderant in Parliament and in the government, either by their influence or by their number.

Their "Creed" was the rights of man. In the name of the "liberty of conscience" they tried to absorb the Church by the "Civil Constitution of the Clergy." Having failed in general, they began a sly and hateful legal persecution against the Church, and pursued her in every domain. Only one power must remain in force in this desert of liberties in ruin, and this must be theirs. Its legal absolutism or Byzantine Caesarism was now praised to high heaven in the name of "free institution," doubtlessly, because the State-God remained unique master over the isolated and weakened individuals of the enslaved, persecuted and annihilated Church.

The work of the legalists was finally codified by Napoleon I, especially in his "organic articles." From that moment the State became "secular," legislation became rationalistic and the expression of the principles of 1789. This permanent Revolution took the deceptive name of "new Law."

When this evil enters legislation, when it becomes the fundamental law of institutions, when it is no longer an ephemeral consequence of a violent passion, but is set up as a system of government, then it is proclaimed as the official doctrine of monopolized education, then it will penetrate every social order, creating a public spirit according to its own image, then it will deprave and deform consciences and will become, humanly speaking, just about incurable.

Later Governments will be unable, or will not dare, to remedy this evil. These legalist principles and their mentality will remain fixed like stereotypes in the code of law and deeply rooted into parliamentary institutions, proclaimed by the press and official education. All this would amply suffice to accelerate the movement of secularization, *i.e.,* universal dechristianization, just in case the antireligious passion should come to an end.

Indeed no government is in itself or by itself bound to the liberal doctrine, but, we must admit that certain institutions have a very special affinity to it. Without doubt, this is because they lend themselves more to the application of its principles concerning authority, liberty, equality and popular sovereignty. Freemasonry also, in its clear perspective, seems to have had a soft spot for democratic republics in Europe as in America. Anyway, governments today, considered in their origins, official doctrine, "hereditary" personnel, legislation and attitude, identify themselves perfectly with the most pure Liberalism. The legalist regime of lawyers has organized the most admirable machine of secularization and legal persecution that we have ever seen.

Even though there have been multiple governments following one another in the last 50 years, we perceive a unique work, clearly conceived and faithfully pursued. The point of departure is always the liberty of conscience, the absolute liberty for man to believe as he wishes or to believe in nothing at all. In this way we arrive invariably at the inevitable neutrality of the State and of all that depends upon it. Both legislation and politics will simply conform to this authentic liberal doctrine.

Unfortunately, by the fact that we live in the contaminated air of noxious liberals, and breathe it into every vein even from a most tender age, Liberalism has created in our compatriots, even too often Catholics themselves, the temperament of the "liberal" sin which no longer allows them to grasp its horror and danger...unless they should return to the principles of sane doctrine and listen with docility *mente cordis* to the infallible voice of the immortal Church.

Chapter IV

THE REFUTATION OF LIBERALISM: "SECULAR" FAITH OR CATHOLIC FAITH

The complete refutation of Liberalism requires a lengthy reply if one wishes to go into great detail or into the multiple forms and applications of this monstrous error. But, as St. Thomas Aquinas puts it: *tota scientia in virtute principiorum continetur*,[1] Liberalism presents itself as a systematic science from the principle of the absolute autonomy of man. It would then suffice to show the inanity of this principle, and, after that to rapidly sketch a parallel between Catholic education and the "liberal doctrine." The exposition of truth and the laying bare of error is the most efficacious apology for the upright intelligence.

The Autonomy of Man—Liberty of Conscience

Radical dependence of man in the natural order. "Either God, or radical absurdity." The existence of contingency in the world is an inevitable dilemma presented to the reason.[2] Reason indeed can prove the existence of a God, creator and sovereign master of the universe. Everything which comes forward as having an evident character of mobility or contingency, evidently does not come from itself but from another, and, can be from no other than from God: He who is. This is the case of the visible world around us of which we are a part. This world is essentially dependent upon the first and universal Cause:

---

[1] All knowledge is virtually contained in the principles from which it flows.

[2] See the conclusion of *De Deo Uno* and *De Revelatione* by Rev. Fr. Garrigou Lagrange.

- **dependent in its becoming**, since God is the first Cause to every real action of secondary causes, without Himself suffering any loss;
- **dependent in its being**, since it cannot subsist even for an instant, without the conserving action of God, who maintains it over and above the non-being;
- **dependent in its action**, since without the motion of God, it can neither begin to act nor continue in its course;
- **dependent in its end**, since it is made for God and yearns after His Sovereign Bounty.

Man in particular, because of his spiritual soul, is immediately and directly created by God and ordained back to Him as his last end. By intellectual contemplation of His essence, man can attain Him, and, in this way also, attain his own ultimate perfection. This brings about both the greater glory of God and his own definite happiness.

Man and the world are therefore essentially relative to God and radically dependent upon Him. These also receive from Him their fundamental law. God, who is infinite intelligence and wisdom, requires the highest degree of glory that this freely created world can render Him by its universal order and harmony. This is why He orders all beings and their activity in view of this supreme end. This universal and essential order of things is the eternal law. It is the principle of divine government, by which God efficaciously moves every being according to its nature, towards its end, towards its perfection, for the progressive accomplishment of His eternal plan. This is the reason why God, who is Order Himself and has put order into the universe, imposes His rule or law upon each being. Inanimate beings have their physical laws, and living beings have their biological laws.

And why should not man, who is the creature with the greatest dignity, because of divine solicitude, have his law also? He is a person, without doubt free, but not autonomous nor independent. He then also will have his law which is conforming to his nature, a law binding his will without violating it, obligatory and non necessitating; this is the moral law. Following this law, the free will improves its own liberty, giving assurance of obtaining goodness and happiness. In the same way, following the laws of justice, the intelligence improves its activity and assures its possession of truth.

Law is therefore everywhere, and, the "submission of the law is the principle of perfection" (A. Compte).

But the fundamental obligations of man required by the moral law, are to recognize God, adore Him, thank and love Him, and tend towards Him as our last and necessary end: This is the first general restriction of this liberty of conscience which the liberals would like as an absolute.

Dependency of man in the supernatural order. If God then elevates man to a higher state by His sovereign independence and gracious bounty, if He calls man to a supernatural life, if He reveals a more perfect religion, if He requires of man a predetermined cult, imposes upon him a destination which goes beyond nature, a destination which man's reason would never have dared to suggest, if He instituted a new obligatory order, then it would be a strict duty for man to tend towards this supernatural end. Man would be obliged to accept this gracious and obligatory gift by submitting his intelligence to the revealed truth in conforming his will to these new commandments. Again another new restriction to the liberty of conscience.[3] This restriction however, limiting the free will, destines to elevate man up even unto the life of God Himself. Now this is an easily proven and historical fact that God elevated man to the supernatural state, and that man, having fallen by Adam, was redeemed and again elevated by God-made-Man, Jesus Christ. From that moment, Jesus Christ acquired the first place in the divine plan by His obedience, and, that man cannot accede to God other than by his submission to the Man-God, in receiving His word, in obeying His laws and the Church, which founded by Him, officially continues His work of redemption.

---

[3] Certain liberals do admit that liberty "must be directed and governed by right reason and therefore submitted to the natural and eternal divine law, but, at this point they believe to have the right to stop, not admitting that free man is bound to submit himself to any law that God may give us through any other way except by way of natural human reason" (Pope Leo XIII, *Libertas*).

How then can one continue to speak about the autonomy of the individual or the absolute liberty of conscience? Without doubt, the supernatural is a free gift, but nevertheless, obligatory. This is not a superabundant luxury or optional thing. This liberty of conscience is something fundamentally absurd. What must be demanded is liberty of consciences in their absolute right to serve God without hindrance (Dom Delatte). Modern liberty of conscience is a postulation that cannot be proven, or rather, is simply a manifest error. What! Man, created from nothing, incapable of being or moving himself without God, with all that he has and is coming from God's bounty; this man can insolently rise up, even in his misery, before the infinite all powerful God, who exists by Himself and by whom everything else exists! This man dares to size himself up to God and even refuse Him submission: it is the height of absurdity.

No, man is essentially dependent upon God, upon His word, His laws, His Providence, His delegated authorities and His societies in which man is placed. Man is dependent upon all laws and ties which protect and save him. This is what Catholic reason teaches, and is certainly more reasonable than rationalism itself. It knows that it must fulfill its principles even to the last one. It knows that it does an act of reason in accepting Revelation, in recognizing the universal royalty of Our Lord Jesus Christ and the authority of the Church.

The supreme principle of Liberalism is therefore wrong—completely wrong! It is even better seen when we compare the Catholic teaching of God-made-man and the liberal doctrine of man who pretends to be God.

Catholic Truth—Liberal Error

It is not true that human reason is the source of truth and measure of all things. In the natural order, the intelligence is submitted to the object, reality, laws of logic and the direction of first principles. The intelligence is measured by things as things are measured by the divine intellect. In the supernatural order, the intelligence is held in submission to the word of God. It has a rigorous obligation to adhere to the mysteries of faith, to listen to the Church and to accept the teachings of the Church.

It is not true that liberty is an end in itself. Liberty is a power that can be put to the service of both good and evil, but, for it to be a right, that is to say a legitimate power, it must submit itself to the order of reason, direction of law and commandment of authority.[4] Liberty is only a means to obtain the end assigned by God. It must therefore be used only to obtain this end and within the limits laid down by reason and faith. Only in this way will liberty obtain that wise Christian definition: "the faculty to adopt the means to accomplish good."

It is not true that man must follow nature, unless it be within philosophic reality, that is, according to the hierarchy of its powers, and in historical truth in as much as it is redeemed and ordained to the supernatural. Once again the Catholic is more of a naturalist than the naturalists themselves. He alone considers nature in its integrity, in the exact order of its faculties and their objects, and in the hierarchy of its tendencies and ends.

It is not true that the dignity of man is such that all dependence is repugnant to him. On the contrary his dignity, excellence and perfection are to recognize the sovereign domain of this God from whom he received his being, to tend towards Him with all his strength, and to perfectly submit himself to His law so that he may possess Him completely. Without mentioning the Christian life, summarized by the virtue of charity, the essence of human life is found in this total and voluntary submission to God: *Deum time et mandata eius observe: hoc est enim omnis homo.*[5] By this humble obedience to God, man also, frees himself from the contingent, the temporal, and from all that is not God. Thus he rises to heights which natural man, *homo animalis,* has not even dreamt about. Does man by his will not assume the quality of the object that he espouses, that which he loves and serves? *Servire Deo regnare est.*[6]

---

[4] "Liberty, this element of perfection in man must strive to that what is true and good" (*Immortale Dei*). Also "Liberty can only be said to be lawful when it sustains our faculty towards good. Other than this, it is never lawful" (Pope Leo XIII, *Libertas*).

[5] Fear God, and keep his commandments: for this is all man (Eccl. 12: 13).

[6] To serve God, is to reign (with Him).

It is not true that man has the liberty to accept or refuse the supernatural gift of grace. God, who made man from nothing, has conserved the right to continue improving His work, elevating man to a more excellent and noble end than what he was in his native condition. In fact, God instituted the obligatory supernatural life, showing the way by clear markers. We are thus obliged to believe in Jesus, in His doctrine, follow His commandments and live a life in imitation of Him. Without this we will completely miss our natural end, since by the actual order of divinely providential things, we cannot attain our natural end excepting it be through our supernatural end.

It is not true that man is free from a social standpoint. Firstly the family into which he is born, or which he has founded, is a natural society of which the constitutions and fundamental laws (unity, indissolubility, paternal authority) were instituted by God, and restored and sanctified by Our Lord Jesus Christ. Civil society in turn was also established by God and all authority therein comes from Him. Finally the Church, a perfect supernatural society, only guardian of religious truth and means of salvation, is obligatory for all men. No one has the right to reject her doctrines or to avoid her laws and authority.

It is not true that the State is independent from God, Jesus Christ and His Church. As agent, it is directly submitted to God. By its own end, it is indirectly submitted to the social reign of Our Lord Jesus Christ and to the Church. In particular, it is bound to profess the true faith, protect and defend the Church, prohibit false cults unless a temporary tolerance is required for the common good of the public, render the temporal and secular power to the Church when she is in need of it, and conform its legislation and practice in harmony with the superior rights of the Church.

Neither is it true that tolerance must be universal. If so, then in the domain of ideas it would cause skepticism, or, in governmental practice it would cause disorder and anarchy. Evil and error can only be tolerated when nothing else can be done.

It is not true, in summing up, **that liberty is a universal remedy.** Liberty must be governed by law which in turn determines her rights and duties, by natural and supernatural prudence which will specify the practical applications:

> We have extolled liberty and its advantages to the skies, and have proclaimed it as a sovereign remedy and an incomparable instrument of peace and prosperity which will be most fruitful in good results.

But unfortunately, facts have shown that a liberty:

> ...granted indiscriminately to truth and to error, to good and to evil, ends only in destroying all that is noble, generous, and holy, and in opening the gates still wider to crime, to suicide, and to a multitude of the most degrading passions.[7]

Let us then no longer confuse true liberty, which is an ordained liberty, with that false liberty which is an anarchical liberty, a liberty of perdition. Far be it for man to think himself absolutely free. He is subjected to all kinds of authority and encompassed by a multitude of titular ties. Conforming himself to order—such is his essential duty and this is the condition which will give him his supreme perfection.

---

[7] Pope Leo XIII, *Apostolic Letter*, March 19, 1902.

Conclusion

Having come to the end of the first part of our study, let us no longer be surprised when we hear it being said that Liberalism is a sin. It is a grave sin of the mind, a sin in itself, for it is essentially a revolt against God and against all order established by Him.

St. Thomas puts it in his very precise terminology, as not only being a *peccatum* but even a *culpa*. A *peccatum* is, generally speaking, a deficiency or a lack of rectitude required in any operation with regards to its own end. In this sense, Liberalism is a *peccatum intellectus,* since it is a gross error and even a contradiction. In its establishment as a system, it destroys itself because it does not recognize any truth nor any good which would have the right to impose itself upon free man. Liberalism becomes a *culpa,* a grave fault, when, and in as much as, it is adopted by the free will of man. In itself it is of "grave or even very grave matter," incomparably greater than the sins of the flesh because it destroys the most important and most excellent of all faculties, the intelligence. It is a truly Satanic sin because it is the only one that he, Satan, could commit and is therefore inspired directly by him. A radical and nearly incurable sin.[1]

But the gravity of the sin of Liberalism is even worsened by the fact that it revolts within its very principle. Because of its independence as a system, if we can call it such, it organizes disorder against all law. Concerning Naturalism and Rationalism, Pope

---

[1] One must be profoundly ignorant of moral theology, if one should be scandalized at this assertion. St. Thomas Aquinas announces countless times the following conclusion: *Peccata carnalia sunt minus gravia, licet turpiora quam spiritualia.*

Leo XIII said that the principles of Liberalism are the "most perverse of all" opinions (*Officio Sanctissimo*).

The following table will make it easy for us to compare liberal principles and their conclusions, with Catholic principles and their conclusions:

For the Liberal:	*For the Catholic:*
1. Reason, source and measure of everything.	1. Reason subjected to its object: natural and supernatural.
2. Individual and autonomous Reasoning.	2. Reason from years of tradition.
3. Autonomy of the will.	3. Dependence upon the law, in regards to good.
4. Atheism or Pantheism.	4. One God, distinct from the world.
5. Man is self-sufficient.	5. God alone is necessary Being.
6. Liberty, an end in itself.	6. Only a means to obtain the last end.
7. Liberty, essentially independent.	7. It depends upon authority, law and order.
8. Independence demanded by dignity.	8. Submitted to the law, source of perfection.
9. Man, essentially good.	9. Corrupted by Original and personal sins.
10. Indefinite and fatal progress.	10. Presupposes order towards the required ends.
11. Equality.	11. Hierarchy and organization.
12. Anarchical individualism.	12. Necessary social ties.
13. License to do that which pleases.	13. Regulated liberty: to do that which is good.
14. Sovereignty of number, or people.	14. Sovereignty of God and those delegated by Him.
15. Free Masonry, *etc.*	15. Catholic Church *etc.*

Thus while Catholicism affirms the absolute subjection of the individual and social reason to the law of God, Liberalism holds to absolute independence. Consequently, it radically opposes the rights of God, Jesus Christ, and the Church. It also opposes the existence of every society, and the temporal good of man and his eternal salvation. This is why we must fight against it in every upright and honest way. There is no time to lose since the evil is great, today more than ever. This iniquity, said Pope St. Pius X, by which "man substitutes himself in the place of God" is "typical of this time in which we are living." Pope Benedict XV: "The undisciplined spirit, which was until now only the sad lot of a few stray sheep, is today inherited by the masses, so that they have upon their lips, that eternal cry of revolt *non serviam*" (December 24, 1919). Only recently an eminent prelate wrote: "At the present hour, Liberalism is the capital error of intelligences and the dominating passion of our age, it causes an infected atmosphere (Pope Pius XI calls it the "pest of Liberalism") which envelopes the political and religious world from all sides. It is a supreme peril for both Society and for the individual. It warps the mind, corrupts the judgment, adulterates consciences, enervates characters, inflames the passions, ties down governments, stirs up the governed, and, not even happy to attain the light of revelation (if that were possible), it advances unconsciously and audaciously upon the light of natural reason and destroys it also."

Even the governmental forces, e.g., the press, education, etc., are in the service of Liberalism. We, on the contrary, have neither money, nor power, nor influence; we are nothing compared to this great evil! Thanks be to God! for otherwise we might have been tempted to confide in ourselves. No, let us have faith in God who made heaven and earth out of nothing, and is pleased to choose the little in order to confound the great. With courage, confidence and serenity, let us follow the Holy Father Pope Pius XI, denouncing secularism and by his master stroke of instituting the Feast of Christ the King, let us preach Christian politics without end. Let us remind the world without ceasing about the indefeasible rights of the reign of Jesus Christ, not only over individuals, but also over all peoples over the entire world, so that He may always be the First, the first in honor and in the exercise of authority.

F. Buisson extolled integral secularism, that is; "the pure and simple application of free thought to the collective life of society." We, in contrast, want an integral Christian order, that is, the spirit of the Gospel impregnated into society, we want to render man the true liberty which is: "to attain his supernatural end by going to Christ." Let us then work without ceasing for the Social Reign of Our Lord Jesus Christ and everywhere proclaim that Christ is King.

"But that is wishful thinking, we are told!" Yes indeed, if we confide in ourselves; not at all, if we take confidence in God and His infinite power. "But would that not cause unpopularity? You will compromise the Church! You have to work with the modern aspirations of the people according to liberty!" For a long time we have known these cowardly objectors who believe themselves to be prudent. On the contrary, they have only managed to increase the universal apostasy of nations.

We reply: We do not help a poisoned man by giving him more poison. It is an antidote which must be given him to save him. Our society is poisoned by the abuse of liberty. It is this abuse of human liberty which is pushed even unto the hatred of the rights of God, which has engendered secularism. And the "pest" by which the world is dying is precisely this secularism. This word comes from the Sovereign Pontiff himself. We then must fight this secularism in all its forms and degrees. This is the only way to save society ravaged by this "pest." It is only upon the ruins of secularism that we can hope to reestablish the reign of Christ, and by this reign obtain peace for the world: *Pax Christi in regno Christi.*

PART II

"CATHOLIC" OR PRACTICAL LIBERALISM

INTRODUCTION: DIVERSE FORMS OF LIBERALISM

In the preceding part, we studied and analyzed the principles and basic essence of Liberalism. We traced its historical and logical development and sketched a quick and brief refutation.

We did show, however, that Liberalism takes on diverse forms following the wiles of persons or circumstance. Rarely does it show itself in all its horror. So that it may be received by inattentive minds, Liberalism ordinarily wraps itself in artistic appearances, even using the mask of truth and virtue.

It is not possible to consider it in all its forms and degrees. This would only prove to be long and tiresome. It would simply suffice to call to mind with P. Liberatore, Pope Leo XIII and Cardinal Billot, the three principle forms it adopts in political and religious orders:

1) **Absolute Liberalism**—This is what we have already exposed. Beginning with atheism and pantheism, it logically concludes the State-God, source of all rights. Its aim is the absorption or persecution of the Catholic Church. It is in flagrant opposition with the rights of God and the fundamental principles of social morality.

2) **Moderated, Mitigated or Semi-Liberalism**—Either it rejects the order of revelation, or, accepting the supernatural at least in fact, it considers politics and religion, the State and the Church

as two orders, two powers absolutely distinct and separate, completely free in their own domain. This is not the brutal formula, "the State above all," but rather an even more dangerous one, "the free Church in the free State," which was first coined by Montalembert. The State, consequently, does not accept the public right of the Church, excepting in view of peace. It establishes a pact of equality between the two powers, making mutual concessions without ever staining the "modern Liberties," which remain the essential basis of the "new right." Normally, however, it continues to tend towards the absolute separation of the two powers. This system logically leads to political and social atheism, and definitively to the contempt of the rights of God and the persecution of the Church.

 3) **Liberalism called** "Catholic" **or practical**—This is the Liberalism which is the subject of this second part.

Chapter I

ORIGIN AND DEVELOPMENT OF "CATHOLIC LIBERALISM"

The Expression "Catholic Liberalism"

From what has already been said about Liberalism, the question must now be asked: can one speak about "Catholic Liberalism"? It seems that these two words, stuck together, are absolutely contradictory. It would be the same as to speak about Catholic protestantism or Catholic rationalism.

If the word "liberal" is taken as meaning the virtue of liberality that stands midway between avarice and prodigality, then every Catholic must be "liberal" as he also must be honest. If one would like to stress that a Catholic, to whichever party he might belong, must show himself a partisan of legitimate and necessary liberties, religious, political, social...then this would be acceptable, even though the word, since it is equivocal, should not be used.[1] The Church has always fostered these liberties. God Himself loves nothing more than that His Church be liberal.

But, if we are to understand this word as developed in the preceding part, as a more or less accentuated protestation against authority, an anarchical independence, a dissolution of necessary ties, then it is essentially anti-Catholic. In this case there is a for-

---

[1] "We wish," wrote Pope Leo XIII, "Catholics to choose and adopt another name for their own political party, so that this title of 'Liberals' which they have sought to call themselves, may not become an equivocal object which may scandalize the faithful" (Cf: H. Brun, p.46).

mal and essential contradiction between these words. A Catholic can only be anti-Liberal, and, a Liberal is logically anti-Catholic.

And yet, during the middle of the 19th century, a certain group of Catholics called themselves "Liberal" according to this last sense. Cardinal Billot, who always expresses himself with theological precision, was obliged to declare that it was impossible to formulate or define into any category at all, this Liberalism of Catholics who went around calling themselves "Liberal." There would be, according to the Cardinal, only one way to distinguish these liberals, and that would be: their perfect and absolute incoherency.

For this reason, we could not really speak about a "Catholic Liberal," or "Catholic Liberalism." This is not a doctrine, but a more or less accentuated liberalism, practically admitted and upheld both by Catholics of good and bad faith. Pope Leo XIII prefers therefore to term it "Practical Liberalism."

Unfortunately, there are many Catholics who are more or less liberal, following this spirit and mentality, and so being affected in their appreciation, attitudes and acts. Although there are many Catholics of this kind, they are nevertheless diversely affected. Equity obliges us to keep in mind, the infinitely different degrees and nuances, going from those who remain good to those who are bordering on apostasy.

Félicité de Lamennais

The Father of this Liberalism, which is called "Catholic," or, better still, "Practical" (Since ordinarily, we cannot admit it in theory), was that unfortunate man Félicité de Lamennais.

Lamennais had more than one thing in common with Rousseau. Both were imaginative and sensual men. Already in his youth, Lamennais was poisoned by the reading of Rousseau, and might even have been raised by his uncle following the method of Emile. Anyway, it is by understanding Rousseau a little, that one begins to understand Lamennais. His doctrine of "common sense," a sort of application of universal suffrage to Criteriology, strangely resembles the instinctive conscience, or, the general will of Rousseau.

Without any serious formation, either in philosophy or in theology, he was struck by the social side of religion, and, immediately announced what would become his "social Catholicism." Incapable of understanding the radical opposition between revolutionary philosophy and Catholic doctrine, he tried to baptize the "social contract," exactly as some Catholics do today. They naively imagine that they can christianize a certain democracy. It will however be the social contract which will democratize Catholicism.

Following the example of Rousseau, he was a fervent disciple of fanatical liberty. In the name of "common justice," he claimed the absolute liberty of the press. If he was *ultramontane* at first, it was not because of some devotion to the papacy, but rather because of a hatred for the Gallican oppression. A little later, he would even revolt against, what he called, the oppression of Rome herself. He dreamt of a haloed democracy of modern liberties, founded upon universal suffrage. Understanding the State according to Rousseau, and, in a modernistic fashion, which is to say, as an executor of democracy, he went about preaching the separation of Church and State, while at the very same time, proclaiming himself an ardent partisan of the union between the Church and democracy.

A certain Catholic historian congratulated Lamennais on his "moderness" We may very well ask ourselves, if this moderness is a good standard? It is absolutely certain, that with his incredible theories on the education of a sovereign people, or on the relations between Church and State, authority and liberty, and, by his tendency to socialism even unto his own condemnation and apostasy, he is the predecessor and super model for certain contemporary "Christian democrats."

It might be understandable to have somewhat of a sympathy for Lamennais or even to plead for him, but, let this not include a justification of his cause. This is what a certain priest did, who was more a politician than a theologian, and more a democrat than a Catholic, when he said: "This great reformer was miserably broken because he sought this movement too soon, this movement which will one day save Christianity in this land" (Fr. Lemire).

The "Liberal-Catholic" School

The so called "Liberal-Catholic" school proceeded thus from Rousseau through Lamennais. It is not surprising therefore, that, vain and brilliant as may be their efforts, they will not stop trying to conciliate contradictory things: God, or the Eternal Law, with a liberty without rule, the Church and the Revolution, the rights of Jesus Christ and the "new rights."

This school however was only founded from the moment that there was a schism between Catholics over the law of the freedom of education in France in 1850. The most prominent members were Montalembert and Mgr. Dupanloup.

We do remind the reader again that there are a multitude of forms and nuances in "Catholic Liberalism." We do not cease to repeat ourselves on this point, so that no one can accuse us of an injustice. These traits which form the portrait of the "Catholic Liberal," such as we have described, certainly do not appear in every mentioned person.

The "Liberal Catholic" is not a uniform type, but rather a "composite portrait" which therefore allows for considerable variations. The "Liberal Catholic" school of 1850-1870 was, generally speaking, less "advanced" than those who shortly preceded or followed the condemnation of Modernism by Pope St. Pius X (1907). Without menacing equity, it would be difficult to treat the early "Liberal Catholics" in the same way as we would treat those recently condemned for their naturalist tendencies, especially a person like Loisy, who was a formal apostate and pantheist.

Nevertheless we have to deplore the fact that many Catholic orators and historians praise these deadly glories, without any necessary reservation. Moreover, we have too often seen different panegyrists exalting and justifying these doctrines or acts, which the Church does not praise. This is perhaps the reason Pope St. Pius X wrote a brief to the nephew of Louis Veuillot on the centenary of his death, but did not allow the likes of it to commemorate the death of Montalembert. There is also a real danger in the appearance of recommending these disputable tendencies, or, even to accredit these formal errors under the guise of talents and virtues. The talents and virtues of "Liberal Catholics" we do not contest.

Nothing is more dangerous than the error of honest people! The purity of a moral life and zeal, even for the Catholic religion, does not suffice to make a writer, orator, a wise man, or a guide of Catholic youth, or, above all, a cleric. I do not know who is more holy: a Cardinal Pie of Poitier or a Mgr. Dupanloup, a Louis Veuillot or a Montalembert, but, there is no doubt that the doctrine of the Bishop of Poitier is much more solid than that of the Bishop of Orleans (Mgr. Dupanloup), and that the Catholic sense of Louis Veuillot surpasses in delicateness Montalembert.

Our aim is certainly not to formulate definite and complete judgments, but only to take note of the "sequence" of the "Liberal Catholic" error during the last century.

Having laid down these preliminary remarks, let us continue our subject.

Montalembert, disciple and friend of Lamennais, began by valiantly fighting for the Catholic cause. From 1850, he began to lean towards a more equivocal Liberalism. At Malines, in 1863, he tried his very best to render the formula which he had learned from Cavour more acceptable, "a free Church in a free State." It was unfortunate indeed, that before his death, he should pronounce, concerning Papal Infallibility, those disdaining words, "Idol of the Vatican." He was also a great admirer of English Parliamentarism, and finally, he turned to Democracy.

Mgr. Dupanloup, principal author of compromise, which was the law of education in 1850, also wished to conciliate the Church with the Revolution. In 1844 he wrote: "we accept and we invoke the proclaimed liberties of 1789" (Religious pacification). With all his force, he favored liberal men and their tendencies. He brilliantly shuffled (the word used by Montalembert) the *Syllabus*, putting in relief that which he did not condemn, but skillfully keeping quiet regarding the principal teaching of the document. By many intrigues and even using the civil power, we see him opposing the definition of Papal infallibility. In politics, he was a partisan of parliamentary monarchism.

Very close to the "Liberal Catholic" school, we find Lacordaire, a converted advocate. Liberal by temperament, and an advanced democrat, he flattered himself in 1848, as dying an "Impenitent liberal."

Something also must be said about Mgr. Maret, professor of Theology at the Sorbonne. He was always a fervent partisan of democracy, not purely understood as a political system, which after all is legitimate, but rather as a philosophical and moral ideal. It was for him a religion whose dogmas derived from the Declaration of the Rights of Man. In this he already saw the necessary and fatal progress of the future. Also, even more than Dupanloup and Montalembert, he was a deep-seated Gallican and staunch adversary of Papal infallibility.

We could cite many other names, illustrious in their own times, but the length of this report does not allow it.

Let us repeat, we do not slight their talents, their devotion for the Church nor their services rendered to the Catholic cause. Neither are we trying to formulate any judgment concerning their persons. If, however, we do not doubt their good intentions, we may nevertheless ask ourselves if the justice of their spirit corresponded to their good will. The putting in relief of this point of view, will help to rectify the too great enthusiastic appreciation of these many and fervent disciples.

At the end of the 19th century and the beginning of the 20th, the "Liberal Catholic" school does not present any name worthy of mention. On the contrary, thanks to the growth of secularism, it has made many recruits by word of mouth, education, the press, both among the clergy and the Catholic people. Was this advantageous to the Church, as they would have liked to believe? We will see in the following pages. Note well, nevertheless, that it is only among these people that we see successively rising....Americanists, Sillonists and Modernists of all degrees. This is already a precious indication of the danger of a certain, even mitigated, Liberalism. These dangers we will better understand when we describe the mentality of the "Liberal Catholic" and perceive his doctrinal and practical deficiencies.

Chapter II

THE "LIBERAL CATHOLIC" MENTALITY

The principal characteristics of the "Liberal Catholic" type of mentality are: an infatuation without reflection for an independent liberty and for novelties, a certain intellectual perversion that mixes and erases the principles, leading practically to a frantic moderation and conciliation of extremes.

The *Syllabus* of Pope Pius IX ends with the following proposition which is condemned: "The Roman Pontiff is obliged to reconcile and participate with progress, Liberalism and modern civilization." The "Liberal Catholic" tries to put into practice that which is not even allowed to the Pope. He wants to remain Catholic without abandoning liberal principles, trying his best to find common grounds upon which he can conciliate these two.

In order that we may understand these vain and dangerous efforts, let us try to penetrate the labyrinth of the "Liberal Catholic" soul. This should be extremely easy since they proclaim to have such a wide, open and generous mind.

What a "Liberal Catholic" is, and What He is Not

The "Liberal Catholic," is certainly not a "Naturalist," nor a Rationalist, but nevertheless, puts a doubt upon the affirmation of the supernatural. Whether he writes the history of the Church, or does a treatise on Patrology, or gives himself to the study of Hagiography, or preoccupies himself with Exegesis, he always belittles and ransacks the supernatural in them.

His naturalist tendencies are specially manifested in political-social orders. "Christian politics" is for him something strange. If it should concern social action, he sees it in a neutral form, supporting interconfessional movements, professional associations, but never as a branch of Catholic action in favor of the reign of Jesus Christ over the world of business. His argument would be, that politics does not belong to a confraternity. Thus little by little, solicitous for numbers rather than for quality, he confines his views to the purely temporal end of these works. He would even go as far as taking the encyclical *Rerum Novarum*, and interpret it according to his own mind. He might direct a newspaper and will regularly suppress the word "Catholic," for the fallacious argument and pretext, that he does not wish to compromise the Church. In reality, he simply uses it to proclaim his neutrality in public affairs. If he happens to be a priest, he retreats from the sublime regions of the supernatural, and prefers to preach upon social issues such as alcoholism or problems of maternity, *etc*. He absolutely loves syndicates, agriculture concerns, *etc*. *Haec oportuit facere et illa non omittere*.[1] This is already a fault of perspective which is one of the traits of the "Liberal Catholic" mind.

He is not a libertine in philosophy, but, is lukewarm towards any intellectual and speculative study, especially Thomism, and even congratulates himself in his ignorance of the last mentioned. He is opposed to voluntarist philosophies, and also to philosophies of immanence, intuition or action. He is quick to point out that moral dogmatism better satisfies modern aspirations. He has a repugnance for Positivism, even in the acceptable part, and also for considerations of reality and even for materialism. He has a soft spot for the Idealism of Kant and his disciples, which is truly dangerous. Because of his horror for the absolute, he inclines towards the philosophies of opinions, mobility and towards a more or less accentuated relativism.

He is no partisan of liberty as an end in itself, nor even as a principle, nor for an anarchical liberty without rule. Yet, he easily exaggerates the excellence of these liberties, warps the use of them, stretches their domain beyond measure and manifests an excessive confidence in the happy results. He certainly does not

---

[1] "These things you ought to have done, and not to leave the other undone" (Lk. 11: 42).

deny original sin, but, in the contemplation of his crystalline and romantic soul, he ends up believing far too easily in the beauty of fallen nature.

In theology, he repudiates, with indignation, being thought of as a free thinker. He is irritated by those whom he amiably calls "caterers of the inquisition," "uprooters of heresies," "bulldogs of orthodoxy," *etc.* At the same time, however, he restrains to the absolute minimum the essential truths having to be believed, the number of defined dogmas, an uncomfortable encyclical, giving as pretext that it was written by such and such a Cardinal, or, relegates with ease in his museum those "antiquities" which he calls "the thesis." In disputed questions, he invokes his full liberty, forgetting the "Catholic sense," that is, the sensitivity of the loving faith, of inclining towards the preferences of Holy Mother the Church. Sometimes he goes as far as to disregard the true nature of the act of faith itself. He no longer sufficiently perceives the motive of credibility in the sovereign authority of the infinitely true and infallible God. Rather, he finds it in "the free appreciation of individual judgment, deeming this belief better than others" (Don Sarda). Consequently the faith becomes a simple "doctrinal preference."

He does not oppose the law, yet he does fear it as he does authority, reducing and challenging it, for, he jealously guards himself against any possible infringements. He is susceptible to the law, disputing and interpreting commandments to his own likings, measuring every drop of his due obedience, unless of course, it favors his own tendencies. In that case, he deforms and even opposes the intention of the law itself. He is not far from considering authority as a lesser evil, and consequently, has a marked tendency to accept it only under the form of "consenting." He takes pleasure in considering liberty and authority as two opposing forces having equal rights, searching with great difficulty, for the assurance of a correct balance between the two. In so doing, he nevertheless does not always resist the temptation to tip the balance in favor of liberty. What he really does not understand, is that the law perfects this liberty in limiting its exercise. Neither does he comprehend the liberating action of authority, nor the fact, that without the assurance of a legislating authority, there could be no legitimate liberty.

As for morality, he certainly is not immoral, having even a liking for devout "moralism," with a smack of Protestantism. He has little interest in speculative truth, whether dogmatic or metaphysical, which forms the basis of morality, crowns it, and, rules it from on high. Hiding the supernatural side of morality which gives it its greatness and solidity, he continues to be ignorant of the hierarchy of values in the natural order of morality. Consequentially, a great importance is given to regulated matter in the virtue of temperance, banishing simultaneously the sins of the mind. A great concern is applied to corporal chastity, even unto puritanism, but, at the same time, unscrupulously mingles the principles, so that the purity of mind is at stake. In the Social order, he pushes the domain of justice so far as to put charity in danger, and, pushes liberty at the cost of obedience to legitimate authority.

He is certainly very religious, even very pious. But his piety is more of the sentimental nature than dogmatic. It is more individualistic than liturgical, tending to pietism, since he is always seeking emotion by means of pious practices. He thus puts himself in danger of a pure sensualism of the soul. Rousseau, together with his romantic disciples, also had a religiosity much like certain more recent immanentists and modernists, all of whom were penetrated by the "divine" into their very subconsciousness. Yet, he, who is so in love with equivocal considerations, also loves, at this point, to invoke a certain unfortunate distinction between private and public life. Very pious in his own private life, he nevertheless wishes to remain neutral in public affairs. This without doubt, so as not to offend the complete liberty of conscience of others. Since religion is an affair of the private conscience, let it not be even named amongst us to condemn, by intemperate affirmations of our beliefs, those who might think otherwise than we.

Neither is he a libertine in the Social and Political order. Oh, without doubt, he nevertheless is often an anarchist deep in his heart. He admits without criticism, the principles of liberty and equality which he really does cherish with devotion. Drawing it to some kind of democratic religion, he practically integrates it with the passionate sway of the people. Finally, with a soul more of a courtier than martyr, he gives in without too much effort to these happy forces.

Neither is he a "Revolutionary," but, experiences a naive sympathy for the "great ancestors," especially for those virtuous "Constitutioners" or "Founding Fathers." He does not know how to defend himself against the equivocal formulas of the principles of 1789. The contradiction and battle between the Church and the revolution, hurts him. It causes him to seek the cessation of this misunderstanding, in curtailing a little, some Catholic dogmas (which he calls "rounding off the edges," or, "becoming all for all"). Appreciating revolutionary philosophy with indulgence, he congratulates himself in uniting them in an embrace of peace, which he definitely hopes are but intransigents that compromise everything.

Neither is he really an "innovator," nor even an adversary to tradition, yet, he certainly has a distinct taste for novelties. This is perceived by the choice of words which he prefers using, such as: youth, dawn, new era, future, life and movement. He does not hold on to the rationalistic dogma of necessary and fatal progress. But he feels obliged to confess that the modern era is incomparably superior to what he calls the inquisitorial and constraining regime of the middle ages. For him, the reign of the "hypothesis" agrees more to the people of today. People today, he says, have outgrown this childishness. They have become responsible adults, tending to a maximum of moral and civil consciousness and responsibility. He is happy to live in such an environment.

Oh no, he does not detest the Church. Yet, often, due to his inveterate taste for a superficial democracy and its liberal mist, he will go about free and easily, sacrificing the rights of God and His Church. He is no enemy of Roman authority, but, now and then, does complain about her negative attitude by which she does not respond flightily to modern aspirations. Generally, he does not directly attack the Pope, but complains that he is a prisoner in his entourage. He does, however, freely attack the Roman congregations. When circumstances are favorable, he accepts with acknowledgment, the favors granted by the civil powers. Without repugnance, he consents to the new "liberties and rights," especially from the moment that these are conceded by a popular and "free" government.

He is no heretic, at least not yet. His love for independence, however, his desire to have an open mind, his taste for novelties; all these things certainly put him on the narrow road to the precipice. It is interesting to note, that of those who were blamed and condemned by the ecclesiastical authority, even from the days of Lamennais until our day, all belonged to the "Liberal Catholic" school. The mentality of this school formed a perfect substrate for error. Let us not forget, nor cease to repeat, that we find in these minds the deplorable success of Americanism, doctrinal modernism, Sillonism and historical modernism, both judicial and social, causing incredible damage, even apostasy. Normally he tries to stop himself half way, or, what he calls, the "happy medium." After having received many a reprimand, he becomes prudent, suspicious, even timid. He thus keeps his distance from the category of formal error, but, retains his weakness for half truths. Similarly to the squid that hides itself in the water by the black liquid that it emits, the liberal conceals himself in a cloud of equivocations and confusions. He thus hides from the inquisitorial look of authority, at least for a little while. Finally, as we have already said, he does not have the Catholic sense, and so, in controversial questions, he tends invariably towards the more obscure part. He is likened to the probabilist or even the laxist in doctrine.

In politics, he does not use the weakness of the people to his advantage, nor does he wish to be an anarchist, but once again, he has a marked liking for parliamentary and popular governments. In that case, he idolizes it since it is an expression of the general will of the people. He loves change in law and government, while he secretly disdains tradition and custom that represent the past. Generally, he does not approve that a priest occupies himself with politics, even to Christianize it, since he fears, what he calls, theocracy and "Clericalism." It is, he would remind Catholics, their strict duty to follow the form of government established in their country, except perhaps, if it is not of a democratic or parliamentary form. This "Liberal Catholic" has a dissimulated veneration for the sovereignty of the people, even a strong propensity for revolutionary liberty. It is strange to see, that with a one-track-mind, he easily sacrifices the truly desirable civil liberty for democracy. He treasures, however, like the apple of his eye, that dangerous political liberty, as also the "modern liberties" of conscience, thought, press *etc*. Absolutely in love with equality, he deplores all kinds of privileges and wraps himself with desires for all to vote. Raging, he bulldozes countries once upon a time "loaded with liberties," with the equalizing rod of "Common Law."

He claims not to be a Socialist, evidently because Rome condemned this together with Communism. Yet before these were condemned, he willingly proclaimed himself a "Christian Socialist," even categorizing Jesus Christ as the first. Today, by the multiplication of laws, he goes about tending towards Statism, seeking the disappearance of class struggle by suppressing classes themselves, and trying to bring them all to a certain unity. He seeks to attain this by means of a corporative and hierarchical organization and by the practice of the virtues of justice and charity. He aims even at the abolition of a salary-structure, so that it may be replaced by the extension of the corporation and the sharing in profits and in control.

He is not in the least anti-patriotic. He loves his country and will even prove it. However, his patriotism is somewhat tainted. He is idealistic, detached from reality, full of his dreams in capital letters expressed as: Right, Justice, Liberty, Progress….From such elevations, he turns away in disdain from the humble "territorial patriotism," and, opposes fanatical nationalism and chauvinism with his wide and generous internationalism.

The Profound Incoherency of "Liberal Catholicism"

These are then the principal traits of "Liberal Catholicism," in which its adherents participate in varying degrees. It is not hard to see that its essential characteristic is the profound incoherence, which the "Liberal Catholic," is not afraid to wear openly, having even adorned himself with it. Yet in this competition of who is left and who is right, he does prefer the title of "Christian democrat." It however brings him no more success, since as we have shown, his democracy is more revolutionary than Catholic.

He believes himself to be a good Catholic, upset if one does not believe in his good sentiments in the religious world. He willingly displays the purity of his moral life, his participation in Catholic works and even his assiduous practice of the sacraments. But, caressing a liberalism in which he is sincere, he tries to prove his goodness in all kinds of ways to those who do not participate in his beliefs. He does his utmost, at least in practice, to conciliate Catholicism with Liberalism, but of course ends up mitigating the one with the other, obtaining a minimized and emasculated Catholicism, or a Liberalism that in the meantime is tolerant and neutralized. Wishing to be both Catholic and Liberal, he ends up being neither the one nor the other. He is too liberal to be Catholic, and not sufficiently Liberal to the taste of non-Catholics. Rejected by the one and despised by the other, he indecisively floats between the two until he crashes down on the side to which he leans; that is ordinarily, to the "left."

Let us not forget that radical incoherence is the character of the "Liberal Catholic." This will serve as a most precious guideline. It will securely help us to wind our way through the labyrinth of his mind and perplexed conscience, so full of mist. It will help to remind us of his mentality, of his apostolic procedures, of his dislikes and even of his constant disappointments.

The "Liberal Catholic" in the Speculative Order

Catholicism has always claimed to bring man an intellectual security in supplying every necessary truth for the direction of life. She brings forward precise affirmations, defined dogmas, determined commandments. Also, she separates every system or doctrine that contradicts her teachings. She does not admit this chaotic syncretism, which does nothing else than seek in many different opinions the "soul of the truth" which may be found in them. She stands up and proclaims to be the only possessor of revelation received from God. Calling upon the reason to guide and direct these truths, she seeks to build an integral synthesis. In this she has always proven her admirable and holy intransigence. Liberalism, on the other hand, is no less rigorous in its own principles and dogmas, nor less determined in its own exclusions. This is ironical, yet a metaphysical and objective necessity that goes beyond their intention. In its own acts, it is determined to exclude any act that may oppose itself.

Nevertheless the "Liberal Catholic" continues to seek a conciliation between the two extremes. Enemy of any intransigence, moderated in principle, he has, above all, a moderate liking for the truth and a mediocre dislike for error. He mixes the upright Catholic with the bad Catholic, composing an amiable gray which is a real masterpiece of confusion.

This is why the "Liberal Catholic" fears definitions. Are they not too cutting, intolerable and anti-Liberal? He keeps his distance from clear affirmations. These would seem to suggest that we can attain the truth, or, be sure of its possession. Consequently he would be obliged to declare as erroneous and false everything that may oppose it. He has a horror of extreme, precise and determined forms, which are, according to him, simple exaggerations. Thanks to a wise equivocal and confused language, he congratulates himself of holding the "just equilibrium"[2] between them. He sees himself standing in the middle of diverse opinions, those on the right and those on the left. While they are fighting among themselves, he most wisely gives his consent only to those in the middle. Thus between being and non-being, he opts for "becoming," between the truth and error, or, between good and evil, he establishes a misty zone. Between Jesus and Barabbas, he would certainly have taken the position of Pilate, yet, on the other hand, lest that would suggest an extreme, he would have put the two, Barabbas the thief, and Jesus the Son of God, on the same plane, executing the same condemnation unto both.

---

[2] "Truth seems to them as an excess. Too wise for the one, too weak for the other, they remain in the middle (we would say: half way) and give to their weakness the name of moderation and impartiality. They forget that if they are to be impartial to men, they nevertheless cannot be in morality" (De Bonald). Truly we can say about them: *in medio stat virus, i.e.*, "Poison stands in the middle," a takeoff on the traditional expression, "virtue stands in the middle," of which liberalism is a faint mockery.

But what a pity! This position that he believes to be moderated, is really nothing but "mediocrity." Rev. Fr. Garrigou-Lagrange wrote:

> Between the evil by excess and the evil by defect,...the good rises above like a summit. Mediocrity is as far from the apex as it is from the opposing vices. He tries to consider himself in the "just middle" when really, he is in a kind of confused middle.

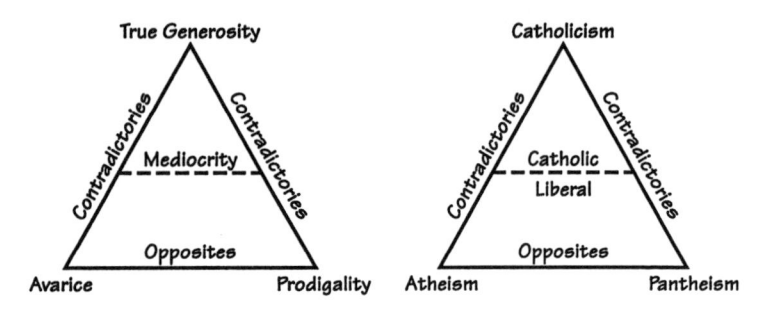

```
        True Generosity                    Catholicism
              /\                               /\
             /  \                             /  \
            /Cont\                           /Cont\
           /radic \                         /radic \
          /tories  \                       /tories  \
         / Mediocrity\                    /  Catholic \
        /-----------  \                  / ----------- \
       /              Co\                /     Liberal  Co\
      /                ntr\             /                ntr\
     /    Opposites     adi\           /    Opposites     adi\
    /_____ctories\     /_____ctories\
  Avarice            Prodigality    Atheism              Pantheism
```

It is therefore an unjust and untenable middle. From the intellectual point of view, the just middle is not found as a halfway term between truth and error. It is found on the extremity, on the summit, in a serene affirmation of that which is controlled by principles, experience and authority. Mediocrity, on the contrary, tries to found itself upon the ground work of existing opinions, whether they are true or false. It seeks to conciliate these by taking some elements, its "soul of truth," from each by an arbitrary choice. This simply ends up floating in a conflagration of confused prattle instead of an ordered synthesis. The wise theologian continues:

> Mediocrity...(appears like) an intelligent mix of truth and error, or a science of good and evil. The mediocre man believes himself to be doing something that God has never been able to do. He seeks to put harmony in everything, ready to mix everything and ends up destroying and confusing everything. He begins to place himself in the center, at an equal distance from good as from the opposing forms of manifest evil. He declares himself a friend of everybody in order to obtain a good standing with as many people as possible. Modestly showing himself off as a wise man, he thinks he has finally been able to conciliate the

diverse aspects of truth and error. So very indulgent towards all variations of evil, he strives even to unite them to good itself. Identifying mercy and justice, as one and the same, he uses it to pardon the impenitent and to attribute to error the same rights as to truth. "Anyhow," he anxiously asks, "does an absolute truth really exist and, if it does, who could boast to possess it?" (cf. *Dieu,* p.733).

Even if he is not too sure why, he at least has the success for which he sought.

> The mediocre man (in fact) obtains an overwhelming success in number....His are the bad, the indifferent...and those whom he tricked. Generally, the vote is his by a strong majority. His opinion is triumphant in those assemblies that are not yet too sectarian. His newspaper will be the most acclaimed in a given region, if, of course, it is still a little Catholic. Mediocrity considers the best authority to reside in numbers, and so, quantity compensates the lack of quality. Thus, naturally, this inclines towards democracy which it transforms into democratism..." (cf. *Dieu,* p.737).

Shortly, then, this becomes a worship of society where the passions of the people hold sway. The sovereignty of God and His laws are simply replaced by the sovereignty of the people and their passions.

Therefore this "just middle" of the "Liberal Catholic" is nothing other than an intellectual perversion, which inevitably destroys the Catholic sense. This we will show shortly.

In short, the "Liberal Catholic" is moderate, nay, rather violently moderate, moderate without measure, even fanatically moderate and ferociously neutral when this may be required. No matter what he does, he inevitably falls into that evil for which he reproaches his adversaries. Thus their own intransigence caused Louis Veuillot to accuse them of being a "sect."

He is very touchy when it comes to his intentions. We attack his ideas; he threatens a lawsuit. We charitably show him that he is mistaken; he is horrified that we put to question his good will. Becoming an enraged lamb, he accuses his adversaries of exaggeration, hatred and violence.

Finally, let us add, that personally he is very intolerant and authoritarian when he certainly could show himself to be more generous. This is logical, since it is the same passion of independence against which he butts when he is required to submit, and which becomes authoritarian when it is a question of command.

The Liberal Catholic in General Practice

In principle, the "Liberal Catholic" does not like to speak about principles. He keeps thus to the field of facts because in this he can more easily use his talents. Yet, already we are obliged to believe that the mediocrity in his taste for truth will naturally drive him to a mediocrity in action (unless the real theory of his justification of attitude is simply his fear of acting and fighting).

Anyhow, we know that any efficacious human act or energetic combat, necessarily presupposes the perception of a good which is sought to be conserved or obtained. This is the whole reason for the effort, otherwise we will react only a little or not at all. The modern world calls this the "law of motivation." One has to deeply love to be strongly motivated, but one loves only as much as one understands the importance or value of the given good. It is then not difficult to understand that there will only be a lukewarm indifference, or at least, a very weak conviction towards truth. It, in turn, engenders a pusillanimity and a cowardice in action. This is but only too often the case with the "Liberal Catholic." Let us add to this that his exaggerated desire for conciliation, together with his weakened faith, causes him to run the risk of making ambiguous transactions and regrettable compromises. These have as consequence shameful retreats, capitulations and an irreparable treason. The last few decades have borne witness to this. Yet, of this, the "Liberal Catholic" believes nothing. He continues, on the contrary, to vent his pride in his so-called solicitude for what he calls a "desire for peace," "prudent conduct," "charitable attitude," "sense of reality," "politics of results." Let us look at these more carefully.

Desire for Peace

The "Liberal Catholic" wants peace at all costs. Yet, this cost is often too high because his conception of it always ends up being at the cost of truth, the rights of God and of the Church.

Certainly, every Catholic must work for peace, that is, for the tranquillity of order in every domain: "Blessed are the peacemakers...." But, as Cardinal Pie explains, peace is only possible in truth because order is only possible if things are disposed among themselves according to the requirements of their mutual relationships. Peace therefore is obtained among men when their activities are ordained according to virtue. In particular, the virtues of justice and charity assure a respect to all legitimate powers and laws.[3] Now, peace is impossible here below between the Church and the world: "My son, when thou comest to the service of God...prepare thy soul for temptation" (Sir. 2:1), "And all that will live godly in Christ Jesus shall suffer persecution" (II Tim. 3:12).

Our Lord clearly predicted this when He said: "you will be hated for my name's sake." This indeed is the privilege of the Catholic who always and everywhere draws a violent hatred and is accused of hypocrisy by the very same world that he condemns. The Church militant will continue to wage war as long as there are souls to be saved. As a result, the peacemaker is often required to prepare for war against the disturbers of order in the battle against concupiscence, the world and Satan. It is because of the love of order and peace that the peacemaker attacks ignorance, error and the passions, so as to save souls. The "Liberal Catholic" on the contrary does not understand the true conditions of peace,[4] which is the permanency of order, since disorder invades his mind as it does even his name. It is the concordance of wills that he desires even above, and notwithstanding, divergence and opposition of minds. The only thing he obtains is a superficial and provisionary tolerance in which the Catholic has everything to lose and nothing to gain. Neither true peace nor esteem of his adversaries is ever obtained by him. Repeatedly you see him

---

[3] These social virtues can however neither be had nor understood other than in the heart of the true religion. Only Catholicism which is the integral order and even the force of God, can by her very nature bring about these to their perfection relative to this world.

[4] Liberalism specifically condemned by Pope Leo XIII, is this systematic concessionism and the passion for peace at any cost (Rev. Fr. De La Taille. *En face du Pouvoir,* p.118).

holding out his hand with an irritating insistence, which we are resolved to refuse with contempt! No, the "Liberal Catholic" is not a peacemaker but rather a pacifist. He has two principle characteristics: an aversion for his Catholic brothers and a perfect understanding with the enemy.

Charitable Attitude

Charity, charity! This is the excuse that the "Liberal Catholic" tries to bring forward. True charity is to love God above all things and one's neighbor for the love of God. These two loves are not separable. We love God and neighbor as God wishes it to be, that is, in the order and in the way which He intended, *i.e.,* by and in Jesus Christ and the Church. True charity knows that the first good is truth; propagating this is thus its first duty. Because we fervently love, we vigorously hate; we vow our inexplicable hatred towards evil, error and sin, and seek to destroy every obstacle that opposes the apostolic mission of the Church. In commenting upon the passage of St. Paul, *facientes veritatem in caritate, accomplishing the truth in charity,* Cardinal Pie writes: "Charity implies before all else, the love of God and truth. It does not hesitate to draw the sword for the divine cause, knowing that only by hard strokes and salutary incisions can the enemy either be overcome or converted." Does the "Liberal Catholic" then love God above all things when he disregards His truths and ridicules His imprescriptible laws? Does the "Liberal Catholic" love his neighbor when he neither helps him out of his errors nor helps him by means of supernatural truths? Does one love the sick when one overlooks his illness instead of healing him? Are souls loved when even elementary truths, which are necessary for salvation, are kept from them so as not to cause them anxiety? No, the charity of the "Liberal Catholic" is badly orientated, when and if it is not completely deformed. He is more of a hypocritical preacher of charity than truly charitable since he is all sugar to the unbeliever, but bitter like gall to the Catholic. His heart is turned to the "left," like his ideas. He has nothing to give to true Catholics other than bitterness and violence. "His zeal is bitter, his discussions sharp, his charity aggressive" (Don Sarda).

Prudent Conduct

At least, the "Liberal Catholic" is "prudent"! He practically assumes its definition, which he created: is it not the virtue par excellence of the "just middle" and the one that regulates all other virtues? With a self satisfying modesty, he repeats over and over again that he never compromises good in aiming idiotically for the most perfect. He rather wisely contents himself with the "possible." But, does that make him all the more just? Prudence is defined as: *recta ratio agibilium,* which can be translated as the "art to succeed," *i.e.,* the ability to attain the end. Prudence never loses its perspective which is the final end of man and the universe. It therefore appreciates every means which will help to attain it. It seeks the greatest possible good in the given circumstance, and yet it considers this only as a stepping stone towards the final end, and not as an end in itself. It takes care of the sick in a useful way, yet it never gives in to evil unless it is bound to tolerate it for the time being, awaiting a favorable moment to triumph even more greatly. Prudence certainly bends to circumstance, but always to obtain a greater good. It labors towards this relentlessly, augmenting every possible good. Never does it sit back resigned to be conquered, but always ends up being the conqueror. It seeks to succeed, never scorning force, but ruling and using it to obtain the end in view. The prudence of the "Liberal Catholic," on the other hand is always vulgar because it is short-sighted, neither seeing high nor far. It falls short of wisdom which is the "knowledge of highest causes." It is feeble and hesitant since there is no conviction in faith. All confidence is spent upon little and mean human ways and none upon God and His grace. This is none other than the prudence of the world, or, a "carnal prudence." The battle, it wants none of, and scorns force in place of putting it to the service of the truth. This kind of prudence only knows how to retreat. Fundamentally, it is none other than fear and even the vice of cowardice.

A Sense of Reality

The "Liberal Catholic" believes and even proclaims himself to be gifted with the "sense of reality," even for want of a

"Catholic Sense." He does not pursue theory but considers himself practical. He claims to know his times, its aspirations and needs. For him, truth must he presented in an entirely new way, to people now maturely impregnated with liberty. He pressurizes the Church to keep an account of progress and to put Herself at its disposition. Yet, this unfortunate person has not the sense of speculative reality, either natural or supernatural, given his incredibly weak love for the truth. Neither does he have the sense of practical reality, since, astonishingly enough, he lacks psychology. He thinks he knows the aspirations of his times, but in reality, is totally ignorant of the profound aspirations of all times, for example, that of the intelligence for universal truth, and, that of the will for the sovereign good. He does not understand the invincible attraction which truth has on every soul. Having far too great a confidence in human ways, he forgets to find succor from Him who made heaven and earth. He neglects the all-powerful grace of Jesus Christ, and has in particular, a very superficial faith in the profound affinity between the sacerdotal soul and the baptized soul. For this reason his sermons, if he is a priest, are inefficacious and dull because he puts emphasis on eloquence and persuasion, rather than on the *virtus Christi*. In place of speaking with authority as representative of God and ambassador of Christ, he makes himself small, humble and suppliant. Consequently he obtains only human success and sometimes even indifference and contempt. He also lacks psychology in face of an obstinate adversary. He thinks that by always surrendering to his adversary, he in turn will receive more, but in actual fact, he loses ground every day. This is what he calls the "possible" and the "lesser evil." Yet, when he makes of this attitude a system, the "lesser evil" becomes the greatest evil of them all, and the "possible" shrinks without end, since the more he retreats, so much the more his adversary advances and holds his ground. This is the history of the resistance of "Liberal Catholicism" for the last 50 years. Thus today we have come to accept and respect the law of secularism! This is the result of such politics. It is heart breaking!

So this feigned "just middle" moves without ceasing, always towards a greater evil. It is remarkable to see how the "Liberal Catholic" has placed himself between the Church and the Revolution. Continually he approaches the side of the revolution and distances himself ever more from the Church. Indeed, in this sense he does advance, continually towards conformity with the people. Is this advancing however in conformity with Jesus Christ? Thus the "Liberal Catholic," whose intention it was to conciliate the Church and the Revolution, has really made possible and facilitated the victory of the Revolution. He has not gained anything from the left, lost much from the right, made no conversions, facilitated much perversion and even caused a multitude of apostasies. He accuses us of endangering the Church, and yet it is She alone who defends Herself before a hostile world, simply by announcing what She believes and wants. On the contrary then, we accuse him of betraying the Church. He puts the Faith in danger by destroying Catholic resistance, or by cowardly forming a pact with the adversary himself. Louis Veuillot quite correctly wrote:

> No group, no notable revolutionary has yet been ever converted by the programs, advances, tendernesses, or unfortunately it must be said, the weaknesses of "Liberal Catholics." In vain have they denied their brothers, scorned their Bulls, and disregarded or disdained the Encyclicals. These excesses only obtained scanty praises, humiliating encouragements and no adhesion. Until now, this liberal chapel has no entry but seems only to have an enormous exit.

The "Liberal Catholic" does not lack intelligence. He has a more perfect eloquence, talent and scholarship than anyone else. It is however his position which is *imbecillus* according to the Latin meaning. In place of building upon the rock, *fundatus supra firmam petram,* he builds upon the moving sands of liberty in which he is swallowed up. His position is totally contradictory since he deplores the very effects of the causes he loves, and, wishes to combat impiety, immorality and heresy without realizing that his own Liberalism conducts him to these very conclusions.

Falseness of Mind

The "Liberal Catholic" has a mind which is completely warped by his own liberalism, and what is worse, he does not even realize this while he haughtily asks you: "What then is an upright mind? Yours I suppose!" An upright mind is the one who humbly conforms to theoretical truth and to practical truth; one who believes what the Church believes, loves what She loves, and, when confronted with controversial questions, inclines towards the preferences of the Church; one who clearly sees by reason and the light of faith, the last end to which God directs all men, and who determines the means necessary to obtain this end from these given facts; one who judges everything according to the Eternal and natural law, and derived positive law. With an upright mind, the Catholic places all things in their hierarchical order according to the teachings of true philosophy and the Magisterium of the Church. Putting it simply, he practices in all things the rule of *sentire cum Ecclesia* (to feel with the Church). Such a mind St. Thomas calls "wise." Wisdom, according to this great doctor, is above all, an intellectual virtue which rectifies the mind, and then only, rectifies the appetite and ordains all its actions. Wisdom is essentially the knowledge of all things, both in the natural and supernatural order, known by their highest and most profound causes, *per altissimas causas*. Since there is no cause higher or more profound than God, Who is both first and last cause, the wise man sees everything from God's point of view which is the sovereign measure of truth in every domain. Such, in contrast to all others, is the vision of the wise man. This is the summit upon which he places his banner and from which he sees every detail, whether it be person, thing, event or action. These things he then always places in their correct respective hierarchy. This is the golden rule of the wise man which allows him consequently to ordain and organize his activity. Finally he brings about order because he knows order: *sapientis est ordinare.*

The "Liberal Catholic" destroys his faculty of appreciation by his confusion of principles, and by his mania for wishing to conciliate the Church and the Revolution with its contradictory doctrines. He no longer judges all things according to God's point of view, nor from any superior view, nor even from the Catholic philosophy of the Church. Consequently, "every moment the clock strikes," he makes a mistake, especially in controversial questions of philosophy, law, theology (in which the

Church has not pronounced any verdict), and in complex questions of history and sociology.

Let us cite a few striking examples:
- He thinks that the proclamation of the Immaculate Conception was ill-timed, yet, the Pope does not heed his superficial fears;
- he disdains the publication of the *Syllabus* of Pope Pius IX, yet, it suppresses Naturalism and Rationalism;
- he deplores that one is even tempted to think of defining Papal Infallibility, yet, the First Vatican Council shows him to be wrong and Catholics are overcome with joy;
- he plunges into exegesis following the modern criteria, yet, contrary to his leanings, the encyclical *Providentissimus* teaches the true understanding of the concept of inspiration;
- he wishes to modernize spirituality and apologetics, yet, Rome goes ahead and condemns Americanism and the philosophy of immanentism;
- he wants to interpret ancient and recent Church history according to his own interpretations, yet, the Church opposes him in this;
- he reminds everyone that all movements must be neutral and interconfessional, yet, the Pope energetically reminds everyone that these must be impregnated with the Catholic spirit. He would certainly have deplored the declaration of the Social Reign of Our Lord Jesus Christ and the condemnation of secularism, *etc.*

We therefore are perfectly correct to repeat incessantly that the "Liberal Catholic" mind is a radically false mind. Let us then not hesitate to discredit him so that he may cease to lead souls astray. Consider, therefore, all his teachings as inferior, narrow and even erroneous. By his teachings, he shows himself to have no right upon the least credit, and even authorizes suspicion. His loves and hatreds are for us most precious indications: Does he accuse a decision? There must be much good therein. Does he congratulate an event? Beware, there must be much to fear in such an event. Does he admire a preacher or writer? Let us sharpen our critical attention. Oh, without doubt, everything he says or does, might not be bad or false, but the "Liberal Catholic" knows how to mask his works with truth and prudence. What certainly is wrong, is his entire perspective which remains silent in important matters and gives a disproportionate importance to minuscule details.

The "Liberal Catholic" Journal

One of the most prominent examples of the error as well as the danger of the "Liberal Catholic" mind, is found in the domain of the press. Its influence upon the formation or deformation of the mind is today extremely profound. The newspaper edited by the "Liberal Catholic," even if clothed with the sacerdotal character, inevitably begins by suppressing the title of "Catholic" so as to reach out, they say, to unbelievers. The fact is that they pervert the Catholic mentality and gain no adversary. "But, does the Church not prescribe the suppression of this name?" Absolutely not. "But would a newspaper with the name of 'Catholic' not evoke a religious authority?" This again is false since the Church always reserves Her authority to Herself. "Would a 'Catholic' journal not be subject to the surveillance of the Church, while a 'political' one escape the control of her ecclesiastical authority?" Again this is false because every newspaper run by Catholics is submitted to the surveillance of the Church and will always remain subject to Her Magisterium, even if it concerns political questions. These questions are always linked to the religious and moral order.

This "Liberal Catholic" journal, or rather, "The Liberal journal run by Catholics" is neutral in both principle and fact.

From the religious point of view, it is neutral: It considers it inopportune and injurious to defend the rights of God and of the Church. It does not hesitate to reproduce *in extenso* the discourse of a politician, but when it comes to a religious document, it freely takes things out of context, if of course it mentions it at all. Religious events are of no interest to it. But if an article does speak about it, it is given some unimportant corner. Even then it is always written in a tendency of alteration and deformation. This is the way that even the least defiant souls are manipulated so as to give practically no importance to something which is the most important: religion. Religion is even put in such a bad light that this often becomes worse than a particular formal error.

For him, neutrality fits in well with the "exigencies of the modern conscience," but, for the exigencies of the Catholic conscience he has no time. Without hesitation he accepts secular laws, mentioning perhaps, some light correction to be made. He energetically reproves any form of "clericalism," and in the name of liberty of conscience, he banishes religion into the recesses of the individual conscience. As a devoted partisan of "modern liberties," he preaches liberty and equality for everyone in common justice. An equal benevolence for all religions and cults is all he asks for from the State.

From the social point of view he is neutral also: Partisan of neutral and "interconfessional" movements, he wants Catholics, "in the ardor of disinterested zeal," to forget religious proselytizing which only divides. They should only pursue a social apostolate which unites. Even the idea of a Catholic Sociology is too much for him. Benevolence, justice, honesty and charity are for him certainly not the privilege of one religion only. He is occasionally favorable to a class struggle by a virulent democraticism, while aiming at social legislation, which, by Statism, will prepare the groundwork for Collectivism.

He takes care not to attack the secular school, whether it be in its principles or formation of personnel. On the contrary, he holds firm that we are to have "confidence in the teaching staff." If he attacks the monopoly of universities, it certainly is not in the name of the rights of God, Church or family. It will always be in the name of "common justice" and liberty of thought, which "is the most necessary of all liberties." Naturally, today he proclaims the secular school, in principle, to be the "only school" and prophesies its immense advantages.

His action is no less dangerous when it concerns the electorate. His objective here is to eliminate all Catholic candidates who are under suspicion of being anti-Liberal. He prefers the amorphous liberal or even the nicely tinted radical. The Rights of Man, which he has finally and totally assumed, becomes the foundation of his politics and the theme of his electoral advertisements. He preaches the absolute independency of politics from religion or any religious authority; no theocracy, no "clericalism": The Bishop in his own diocese, the sacristan in his sacristy, and he himself in politics; above all, democracy according to the sense of 1789. He certainly would never rebuke any legislation which is in concordance with his principles. By always speaking favorably about them, he seeks to slowly make them ever more acceptable.

The history of his desires and aversions is very significant. He began by voting for the Civil Constitution for the Clergy; then at a suitable time, he declares himself favorable to the separation of Church and State and to acceptance of the cultural associations for the administering of the Church (condemned by Pope St. Pius X in 1906). In the time of their success, he manifests a particular esteem for the "bold" philosophers and "audacious" exegetes. Naturally he favors the Sillon, even breaking his neck for it. The condemnation of the Sillon causes him to break out in a rage, he the great moderator, who is softness itself. He enters an alliance with the panegyrist and even the printer of the most doubtful newspapers, often edited by Catholics or priests with strong modernist tendencies. When, in 1917 the Russian Revolution broke out, so did his profound anarchism, while he prints his great and exuberant joy in bold letters. Contrariwise, Mussolini vigorously breaks down parliamentarianism and he cries with accusations of despotism, adding every calumny he can find. Now suddenly the battle against the constituted power is out of the question. He declares himself an intolerant enemy of all intolerances, no matter from where they may come. This of course puts him in a difficult position vis- à-vis the dogmas of the Church and the ecclesiastical Inquisition. Resolutely optimistic about the adversaries of the Church, he remains bitter against anti-Liberal Catholics and vows a grudge against them. He considers them as destroyers of upright minds, and even the most dangerous enemies of that church which he claims to serve. Unfortunately, in reality, he only uses her to obtain his own political ends.

In conclusion, all his judgments upon events and men are impregnated with the most pure Liberalism. A typical mark of his, is the total absence of a "Catholic sense." Normally, however, you will not find clear errors and formal heresies in him, because he knows that he is being watched. Though he lacks supernatural prudence, he does practice it according to the children of this world. With him there is constant vagueness, equivocal statements, calculated dosages of half-truths, false appreciations, slanted or even lying information. But should we belie an error once committed, he retaliates perfidiously and obliquely or with calculated silence. All of this is much more dangerous for the mass of little informed minds than an open error or even violent anticlericalism, because it slowly creates a deplorable and tenacious mentality. "It smells of heresy," Louis Veuillot would say of him. While he waits, he continues to create a cradle for radicalism in his region. He lulls unbelievers into a most dangerous indifference and produces disquieting ravages among Catholics by very suspect notions and maxims. Concerning him, we can very well repeat that famous saying: "My God, deliver me from my friends, but as for my enemies, I can look after them."

Chapter III

THE RELATIONS OF CHURCH AND STATE ACCORDING TO THE "LIBERAL CATHOLIC"

The profound incoherence of the "Liberal Catholic" is manifested even more when he speaks on the subject of the relations between Church and State. He goes about this with particular affection, using all of his many talents, and infinite flexibility. Again, his point of departure is false and illusory. He wants peace at any price, even at the cost of souls and the Church. Firstly he scorns the plan of God, or at least, holds it in no regard. It is the dignity of the human person and his most sacred liberty which screens the rights of God and His Church. He conceives the State very much like Rousseau, seen through the eyes of Lamennais, as a certain executor of a certain democracy, which, according to true philosophy, is the holder of divine authority and organ of the common good. Having therefore no idea of the true nature of the Church nor even of the State, it is impossible for him to determine a suitable mutual relationship. This regularly causes equivocal and confused solutions, compromises and transactions that normally damage the Church, and even the State itself.

The Catholic Doctrine—The Divine Plan

The first truths that appear in the plan of God concerning man are: Man was created by God and elevated by Him to the supernatural life. Man fell by original sin but was redeemed and restored to his original dignity by Jesus Christ who became the one and only mediator. Finally man is called to the intuitive vision, in and through Jesus Christ. The Church was instituted by Jesus Christ to continue this work of the Incarnation and Redemption. By Him, the Church was sent on a mission to all nations to bring back the sheep, lost through error and vice, so that they may be united as living members of the mystical body of Jesus. Thus the role of the Church is to complete and perfect Jesus in His predestined members of this world.

The Church is a spiritual society of positive and divine right, continuing the Incarnate Word, having as her essential last end the salvation of souls and eternal beatitude. So that she may attain this end, the Church has received from the God-Man a suitable organization and the necessary powers which makes her a perfect society in all these domains: legislative, judicial and executive. Her immediate domain concerns souls and spiritual things. Yet this extends also to the body and temporal things in as much as they touch the aforesaid, and of this, the Church is judge alone.

The State is a temporal society founded upon the demands and needs of human nature, and is of divine, natural and positive law. Its aim is the temporal common good of its subjects or citizens, this good consisting in respect and security of law (*pax*), and the abundant sufficiency of necessary and useful goods for human life (*prosperitas*). The State has received from God, its author, a sovereign authority, so that it may efficaciously attain its end. Its domain, powers, rights and duties are therefore determined by its principle, the authority received from God; and from its aim, the temporal common good of the civil society over which it presides.

Even though these two powers are independent and sovereign in their own respective domains, they necessarily meet at each instant, since both have the same subjects. The Church affects the body through the soul, and politics through morality and religion; the State affects the soul through the body, and morality and religion, principle elements of common good, through politics. Thus, there exist inevitable and necessary relations between them. These are determined by origin, nature and the ends of the two societies. From all points of view, the Church possesses the supremacy.

The State is subject to the Church like the body is to the soul, like the reason to the faith.

The end of the State is certainly not of itself ordained to the aim of the Church, however it must not oppose her. The State must nevertheless, in its pursuit of its own end, prudently favor the aims of the Church according to her needs and desires. Therefore, civil legislation must be established in perfect harmony with that of the Church. Practical politics must be inspired by her mind and conform itself to her attitude. In this well ordained system of relationship, the State will be Christian, and the Church will have a preponderant and privileged situation. All rights are protected, all ends are assured, and man, embraced, protected and guided by both societies, sovereign but subordinated, the Church and the State, moves forward with assurance towards his eternal happiness. The gospel rules the State and in the world there is the peace of Christ in the reign of Christ the King.

Such is the ideal order and harmony founded upon the will of God and the nature of things. Whatever may be the circumstance, the Church invariably proclaims this order and tends towards it relentlessly with a supernatural force and prudence.

The Practice According to History

The conduct of States however has varied greatly in time. The pagan Caesars began a bloody persecution, while the apostate or heretical Caesars caused a hypocritical persecution. In the time of the Protestant reformation and the 1789 revolution, a regime of absorption and persecution of the Church by the State took place in different mission countries.

In the 19th century, under the influence of "Philosophism" and "Rationalism," a system of an absolute separation of Church and State was invented. Henceforth, the two powers would have to live side by side without hindering each other, or rather, without even knowing each other. This is the atheistic and social politics of the State, a negation of the essential rights of God and of Jesus Christ, a negation of all Christian politics, as destructive to the State as to the Church herself. In many regards this last system is more pernicious than the aforementioned, because that first system produced glorious martyrs while the last only brings about apostates.

Sometimes however, the State did understand its duty towards the Church, and consequently formed its politics and legislation according to her teachings. This caused an efficacious, prolific and beneficial protection for the Church. This was the insertion of the divine right into the public right of the people. The Church remembers with gratitude, men like Constantine the Great, Theodosius, Charlemagne, Sts. Louis, Ferdinand, Stephen and Edward, and, only a little while ago, a great leader of a small country, Garcia Moreno. Unfortunately this protection sometimes degenerates and becomes oppressive and corruptive. This is not due to the system of indirect subordination of the State to the Church, but because of a defective application of this excellent theory by the State. Yet, even in times of abuse, it leaves behind immense advantages.

In our day and age, given the profound division of consciences, the regime of civil liberty of cult, or tolerance, had to be instituted. "The civil liberty of cult is the faculty by which the State allows citizens, to choose and practice their religion, in all security, under the protection of law." The Church then establishes, together with the civil authority, a Concordat that determines the measure of tolerance and a proper legal situation. This Concordat does not imply equality, nor the renunciation of the Church's own rights. It creates concessions, sometimes even great, in view of avoiding greater evils and obtaining a greater good. The Church, always keeping in view her essential end, the salvation of souls, prudently bows down to circumstance and draws the best possible part from it. Never does she neglect, however, to tend to that end for which she must strive. Though the Church keeps faithfully to the stipulations of the Concordat in its duration, the State has often unscrupulously violated and abused it.

The Attitude of the "Liberal Catholic"
—The Thesis and the Hypothesis

The "Liberal Catholic," filled more with memories of the doctrine of the Revolution than the teachings of the Catholic faith, opts for the regime called "modern liberties," or, political and social atheism born from Rationalism. Both Popes Gregory XVI and Pius IX condemned, ceaselessly and pitilessly, this theory of absolute separation that excuses the State from all its duties to God and the Church. Causing indifference, it simply leads to persecution.

Despite this condemnation, Montalembert, long standing disciple of Lamennais, repeated at Malines in France (1863), the liberal thesis under the formula of "A free Church in a free State." Though applauded by Liberals, this orator was immediately condemned by Rome. To save him, Fr. Curci invented his famous distinction of the "Thesis and Hypothesis" (*Civilta Cattolica*, October 17, 1863):

> If we are to speak about modern liberties as a thesis, that is to say, as a universal principle, applicable to all times and all countries, founded upon human nature itself and upon the divine plan, then these liberties are absolutely condemnable and have been condemned as such many a time. However, if we are to speak about them as a hypothesis, that is to say, as an appropriate disposition to the special situation of such or such a people, then they may be legitimate and Catholics can love and defend them.

This was the saving element for "Liberal Catholics." The *Syllabus*, published in 1864, caused confusion among "Liberal Catholics." Mgr. Dupanloup, however, reminded these last mentioned, of the distinction between the "thesis and the hypothesis." He tried to show that the pontifical document aimed only at an ideal society that has never existed. "Liberal Catholics," he therefore claimed, should not change their attitude at all because they were not in a thesis but in full hypothesis. This explication of the *Syllabus*, although done with respect, reduced it to very little if anything at all. Pope Pius IX, while he filled the bishop with praise, was not fooled when he expressed his desire; "if he (Mgr. Dupanloup) would give more care for the correct interpretation of this act (the *Syllabus*), then he would automatically refute with greater insistence any false interpretations."

As from this moment, the "Liberal Catholics" felt reassured. They, in fact, accept the doctrine as thesis, but since they consider themselves exclusively in the state of the hypothesis, they therefore consider themselves sovereign and infallible judges. No pontifical condemnation can now touch them:

> They deem themselves excused and in order with the Church because they accept her doctrine theoretically. Equally excused and justified to abandon the defense, sacrificing it to the domain of action from whence they retreat from the duty to affirm it. Under the pretext that they occupy themselves with the relative and the concrete, they separate that which they call the absolute or ideal design. They make everything of the hypothesis and leave the thesis bare (Barbier, I, p.60).

Thus little by little the thesis is relegated into a world of ideas, soon into some myth, utopia, completely separated from the real world. Following this they conduct themselves as if the thesis no longer exists. In conclusion we see Catholic orators and ecclesiastics of every degree, having had their fill of Congress, proclaim from on high that the regime of exceptions, privileges and immunities has come to an end. All we want, they say, is "liberty and equality in common justice." To this they add in naive confidence: "It is the simple logical conclusion of the liberty of conscience."

Pure naive confidence, since these poor unfortunates do not seem to doubt that Freemasonry wants nothing other than to reduce the Church and all Catholics to the common right even in the very name of liberty of conscience. By common right, however, they postulate a system in which all right is derived uniquely from the general will of a sovereign people, which is the State, source and measure of all right...and this, by the "liberty of conscience." This is nothing other than the so-called right to disbelief or simple atheism, which is totally contrary to both a religion of the State and Catholic politics!

Thus the "Liberal Catholic" thinks that he is in accordance with his adversary, the Freemason, since he uses the same verbal expressions. Is it possible to be so grossly mistaken? Does he praise himself because he has reduced his adversary's pretensions by such shrewd arguments *ad hominem*? Unfortunately it is he, great liberal Catholic that he is, who ends up sacrificing necessary principles by the weakness of his own intellectual position; it is he who is caught in his own trap that he believed he set so well.

Whatever it may be, we are obliged to recognize here, one of the most dangerous forms of liberalism: To want to substitute Catholic law with an equivocal common law.

In virtue of their own principles of liberty, equality and sovereignty of the people, "Liberal Catholics" neither like speaking nor hearing about a "Religion of the State." On the contrary, they enforce the liberty of cult without distinction. Not even trying to hide their preference for the separation of Church and State, they specify simultaneously the union of Church and democracy.

Pope St. Pius X had a profound understanding of the rights of God, the rights and needs of the Church and even of society, and so solemnly condemned the law of separation in its principle as well as in its name (1906).

Notwithstanding this, our "Liberal Catholics" did not even consider themselves beaten. If they simply claimed that a regime of separation was better and preferable than a regime of violent oppression and persecution, or even accidentally, to a concordat, interpreted and applied by a government hostile to religion, then perhaps we would have been able to come to some mutual understanding. But they go far beyond this. Without doubt, they do acknowledge that the union of Church and State is preferable in principle, but in fact, they claim it to be impossible. When they speak on the subject of history for example, they insist upon the great difficulties that came about from the protection of the Church by the State (at least if the State was guided by an absolute monarch). At the same time, they carefully avoid mentioning the great advantages which issued from it. On the contrary, they seek to vividly expose the immense benefits coming from liberty and separation. "Modern aspirations," they claim, require an ever greater *modus vivendi*. "No longer bothering at all about the absolute thesis, which is totally impractical, they ("Liberal Catholics") want for themselves and the Church equality in liberty. Also they are resolute never to expel their adversaries from the common right, for they believe that the day shall come when their cause will triumph" (Fr. Klein, *Nouvelles Tendances en Religion et en Litterature*, 1898).

From our side, we could understand the "thesis-hypothesis" distinction correctly, under the condition that: the "thesis" be the theory that enlightens, the end which attracts and motivates; and that the "hypothesis" be the practice and means. But these two could never be separated. Truly, the theory is the light, director and aim of the practice that flows from it, the prudent and progressive application of herself in given circumstances. Yet, it must never be forgotten, that it will always and only be the hierarchical Church who reserves to herself the judgment of these same prudent applications. Finally, the condition which sums up all conditions, is that this entire process can only be used by minds completely devoid of the least trace of Liberalism.

But here precisely lies the problem. The "Liberal Catholic" corrupts and stirs together everything, theory as well as practice. His results can be seen as follows:

a) He separates the theory and the practice.

For us, according to the language of the liberal school, the "thesis" is simply the form which is first desired as an end. It is brought about ever more in the matter, which is consequently disposed more and more to the form. Wisdom helps us know more perfectly the hierarchy of ends desired; speculative-practical science gives us the theory of the means to be used in order to obtain these ends; prudence enlightens our understanding as to the immediate use of the best means so as to best attain *hic et nunc*, the constantly desired ends. Thus every cause is called upon to contribute its share, from pure speculation even unto the humble practical execution, everything is joint, every step is linked.

The "Liberal Catholic" goes about separating the end from the means, or, the theory from the practice, and still worse, opposes them, such as to render them incompatible. For him, the "thesis" is an impossible, synthetic and abstract "ideal"; the "hypothesis" is a concrete and real "possible." He has a mania for certain imaginary oppositions:[1] Just as he opposes authority and

---

[1] Would it not be better if we simply have recourse to the accurate scholastic language, rather than cause so much confusion? In this case, the "thesis" will be:

liberty, so also he willingly claims that the partisans of the "thesis," are unable to bend to the "hypothesis," that the speculatives are not able to be practical, having no sense of reality, and, that intransigent doctrine cannot conciliate with practical prudence. He, the "Liberal Catholic," reserves the "absolute triumph of principles and the integral realization of the Catholic principle for blessed eternity." For the present, he encases and collects defeats with a continuity which would have been touching if it were not first of all heartbreaking. He is blind to the fact that between the abandoning of the thesis and the immediate putting to practice thereof, there is, this time, a "just" middle, which is simply to want it constantly and put it into practice as soon as possible in the given circumstances. Instead of first looking at the "thesis," which is to say, the desired end and the general and particular rules for its application, all which supplies the theory, and then simply affirming them and putting them to practice in a prudent manner, he encloses himself in the obscure complexities of individual cases, being even hypnotized by the practical difficulties of the "hypothesis," and begins to belittle and even dissimulate the "thesis." Thus, it is no longer the theory which rules and guides the practice, but the practice which becomes the measure of the theory.

The "Liberal Catholic" cannot stand to hear an announcement, for example, on the conclusions of the public rights of the Church. Confusing the necessary affirmation with the immediate and brutal realization thereof, he quickly considers them as

---

A) The **final cause** (motor), the end desired by suitable means.
B) The **extrinsical formal cause** (director), the model, exemplar or ideal which directs the agent in his activity.
   The **theory** would supply the end, the means and the more or less general rules of application: a domain of science.
   The **practice** will choose the means to better bring about the ideal in the different circumstances: a domain of prudence as well as the "hypothesis."

"outrages thesis," good perhaps for seminaries, but inapplicable to the real world.[2]

He continues: In principle only truth has rights, yet, in practice, general liberty will bring more good than the protection of the truth. In theory, it's the union of Church and State; in practice, we must aim for their separation. Really, the Catholic right will be nicer, but, in fact, common right, which is in greater conformity with modern mentality, will bring more substantial and tangible fruit. It will make, by its superabundance, the divine vitality of the Church more conspicuous...

So the "Liberal Catholic" also makes a theory, but it is a false theory which he tries to put in the place of common sense and the Church. Because of such reasoning, he disregards, forgets and scorns the "thesis," and by consequence, he no longer knows what he wants nor wants what he must. No longer knowing what he must admit or maintain, what he must reject or fight for, worried on the contrary of any conciliation with extremes, he is on the road to those capitulations which fatally end in renunciation and treason.

St. Thomas Aquinas, our guide, takes not the least notice of the "thesis-hypothesis" distinction. He only knows the speculative

---

[2] "It is obvious," wrote Fr. E. Barbier, "that it would be an exaggeration and an imprudence to push for the integral affirmation of directing principles of Christian politics in every manifestation of social and political action. An electoral program or a parliamentary discussion would by necessity require certain considerations and transactions. However, if there is time for silence and discretion, there is also a time to speak because a total silence would be the same as an abandonment: if there are concessions to be made in practice, there are also principles to be safeguarded since they are the source of right which we can in no way neglect."

"It is already well," wrote Fr. de la Taille, "not to find the secret of this temperament which requires from the thesis only that which the hypothesis supports, in the effacement of principles and still less in their alterations. If there are any sacrifices to be made, they are not made on the principles, nor by consequence, upon the future ideal, but only upon the exercise of a right or prorogation for which public interest requires its temporal abandoning." These prudent transactions are finally, in short, the best way to cause the triumph of the "thesis" itself.

intellect which contemplates the truth, the practical intellect which ordains the truth to action, the appreciations which measure and rule the volitions and actions. Once a suitable or obligatory end is known and efficaciously desired (intention), it determines the judicial choice and prudent use of the means (election).

He certainly would not understand why we would want to separate the means from the end, prudence (rule of concrete acts) from science (more or less universal principle of action), practice from the theory.

A businessman wants to make a profit—that is his end; he considers the best means to obtain it—the theory. The end and the theory would make his "thesis." He is not going to stop considering his end and informing himself by the light of the theory, when he puts it all to practice in executing his plan. Thus, his prudence, enlightened by his knowledge, and keeping in mind the present circumstances, will slowly, methodically and progressively cause that first desired end. It will be foolhardy for him to neglect the factual circumstances, or not to know the principles of economics, and, it will be absolutely absurd for him to reject his aim.[3]

The same is the case of the priest, who, moved by the love of God and souls, wants to bring individuals, families and nations under the necessary and beneficial yoke of Jesus Christ. Such is the end for which the obligation weighs upon him all the time, for which he measures its extension, for which the best acquisition is aimed at. To accomplish it, he needs to know two things: firstly the rights of God and Church, the ideal of the Christian city, and secondly, the needs of man, his psychological and historical conditions in which he finds himself. Armed with this knowledge and strong in this love, he will not cease to remember the saving principles with a holy intransigence and prudent charity. To promote this Christian city, he always seeks to bring it more and more to reality by bettering the circumstances, but always under the constant direction of the hierarchical Church.

---

[3] "For things that are desired as means in themselves, the whole reason of wanting them comes from the ultimate end" (St. Thomas Aquinas).

Therefore, there is no opposition, not even a "hiatus," between the theory and practice. If one were to object that the "thesis" no longer responds to "modern aspirations," he will reply that we are then to work upon these aspirations in modifying and reforming them, knowing that the "thesis" always corresponds to profound aspirations, to the essential needs of humanity. Its absolute rights do not depend upon the subjective acceptation of the individual. It then always remains necessary to recall the "thesis," to let it shine before the eyes of all, and if in practice it might not always be expedient to say the whole truth, it is however never allowed to be diminished or contradicted. The best way to let the "thesis" triumph and be loved, is not by dissimulating it or keeping quiet in its regard, but by making it known. We must manifest the truth, its obligation, its beauty, making it desirable and bringing it into practice as much as possible, relying more on the force of truth and God than upon small-minded cleverness or miserable human knaveries.

Fas est et ab hoste doceri,* remarks pagan wisdom, and, the Incarnate Wisdom does not hesitate to give us an example of prudence from the sons of this age. However, the most perfect example of the application of the "thesis" is given to us by modern Freemasonry. With what methodical perseverance, with what audacious guile have they not introduced in our country this universal secularization. This Satanic plan of theirs was elaborated in their dark lodges! Their great method was to attain the government itself, and through it, the entire legislation. The crowning of it all, is that they far too often succeeded. Their formulas and principles were greatly accepted, even by their adversaries, the "Liberal Catholics."

It is time that the Masonic intransigence be opposed with holy and Catholic intransigence, that their guile be opposed with a prudence enlightened by the Spirit of God, force, truth and love.

No, the calling to mind of the "thesis" is never untimely. No, the practice must never be separated from the principle; it must

---

* [Translator's Note] *Fas est et ab hoste doceri*—*It is lawful to learn from one's enemy.*

be brought to light. In this way we will indeed accommodate the Church to our age, as it is said sometimes. But, never may we do so by sacrificing the truth for error, the rights of God for the caprices or passions of man. It is not by correcting the doctrine according to the wiles of the age or according to the liberal method, but by reforming the tendencies of the age[4] to the requirements of doctrine. This is the only Catholic, efficacious and common sense method.[5]

---

[4] In this sense, we could say with St. Paul: *Nolite conformari huic saeculo*.
[5] For a better understanding and rectification of the distinction: "Thesis-Hypothesis":

In the Speculative order:
Contained in this order are the truths in which the mind finds its rest when she contemplates them. It is defined as: *per conformitatem intellectus ad rem*. These most general truths are given by wisdom, either natural (metaphysics), or supernatural (speculative theology).

In the practical order:
Contained in this order are truths which the mind uses in order to accomplish other works. It is defined as *per conformitatem ad appetitum rectum*. i.e.: by the conformity of the appetite to the will already rectified by the love of the true end. These make up the practical knowledge. This knowledge however is made up of degrees. The following is their distinction:

    a) **Speculative-practical knowledge:** The hierarchy of ends desired; general principles of action and universal conclusions. (general morality, Philosophy and Theology of Law).
    b) **Practical knowledge:** More and more particular principles and their conclusions. (particular morality, Pastoral, Casuistics, Law, etc.)
    c) **Practico-practical domain:** This concerns the operating individual. In this domain we have a greater universality, therefore more knowledge. Here it is prudence which is given the charge to direct and bring about the desired end by proportionate means, by the light of principles and according to the occasion that circumstances may require.

The modern use of the "hypothesis" would therefore best correspond to the "practico-practical"; the rest belongs to the "thesis" or theory.

b) The "Liberal Catholic" attributes only a theoretical value to the teachings of the Church.

He believes himself to be in good-standing with the Church because he accepts her teachings. Yet he does not believe that he should change his practical attitude in the least. This new sophism, Fr. Barbier refutes in the following way:

> No, it is not correct to consider the teachings of the Church and those acts that she thinks are opportune or necessary, as simply speculative or theoretical in value, nor to consider them as aimed only at doctrine and not at their application, at the thesis and not the hypothesis, at philosophical or political systems and not at existing constitutions or legislation.

The Church certainly does consider the difficulties of the present state of society, but teaches the doctrines that are not to be forgotten, the conduct to be followed in present circumstances and the plan which Catholics must seek to bring about. She admonishes them to put her doctrine into practice as much as possible.

When the Church teaches her power and rights, she does so regarding the truth in the practical order which belongs to morality. These are rules concerning the conduct of governments, people as well as individuals. To reject them and drive them into the domain of the ideal under the pretext that they are not made for the real world, is the same as denying them.

c) Regarding tolerance. The "Liberal Catholic" confuses the duties of the chiefs of State and those of the Catholic citizen.

Tolerance is essentially a political and prudential act. Whoever governs is often held to tolerate certain disorders in order to prevent a greater evil or to conserve a greater good. The Catholic Church and God give the example. The State too, is sometimes required to tolerate certain errors or evils for the common good, for example, the existence of religious sects. It must however protect and favor only the true Church.

The Catholic citizen does not practice this same tolerance. On the contrary, with all due respect to rights justly conceded, he works with all his strength to exterminate error, opposes its progress and denounces its evil deeds. He must work for the integral restoration of the rights of God and the Church by affirming and courageously defending them.

d) The "Liberal Catholic" freely imagines the Christian right to be a pure myth.

This imagination, born from pure laziness, also comes from a lack of faith and confidence in God. What is impossible to man is possible to God. The marvelous progress of the new-born Church in spite of the formidable organization of paganism is ample proof. Nobody, not even among the intransigents, will hope that modern society is going to find its way to Damascus by a sudden reversal and integral acceptance of Catholic right. But is this a reason for not striving after its ever-so-slow progressive triumph? Is this a reason we should accept principles which contradict Her because of some anxiety for peace and conciliation? Le Play wrote:

> I know of nothing more dangerous,...than those people who propagate false ideas under the pretext that the nation will never renounce her plans. If she does not renounce them, she will perish; however, this is no motive for us to adopt these errors so as to accelerate her decadence. There is no other rule of reform than to search for the truth, to confess it without reserve whatever may happen...

And then, let us repeat with Cardinal Pie, this Christian right, which was the right of Europe for a thousand years, can it not again be adopted? What indeed is synthetic and truly evil, is a social order built upon disorder, upon error, upon an anarchical liberty which constitutes the "new right."

But we would never end if we would have to dispute one against one these sophisms by which the "Liberal Catholics" try to excuse their culpable feebleness and mitigate their defections.

Let us, in finishing this paragraph, at least recognize that this distinction of "thesis-hypothesis" becomes far too familiar with the "Liberal Catholic." With it comes his defeat rather than his victory, because of the radical falseness of his intellect, lack of faith and Catholic sense, a falseness which is both a convention and a fabrication, an ambiguity and a danger.

Thanks however to this distinction, "Liberal Catholics" believe themselves well established and sheltered from all condemnation. While accepting the Catholic doctrine, the "thesis," they tranquilly continue to practice the "hypothesis." Pope Pius XI energetically tarnished this attitude as "practical modernism":

> These same,...who profess this Christian doctrine, act in their discourses, writings and in their whole manner of living, as if the teachings and the orders (of the Sovereign Pontiffs) have lost their original force or even fallen completely in disuse....Here we have a new gender of moral modernism, juridical and social, which we must recognize and which we condemn with all our strength and all our soul as we condemned dogmatic modernism (*Ubi Arcano*. 1922.).

Separation of the Public and Private Domains

These two new distinctions invented by "Liberal Catholics," come from the modern concept of "the liberty of conscience." Without doubt, the "Liberal Catholic" does not explicitly claim that every person is free to believe or not to believe as he may wish, but he acts as if he does admit it and this through a sort of practical modernism.

Lightly infected by naturalist and rationalist venom, he lacks a firm foundation in the faith. In place of putting his confidence solidly in the evidence of truth or the authority of God, in place of considering the authentic marks and manifestations of truth which Catholicism presents, the "Liberal Catholic" is tempted to believe that the objective truth depends upon the subjective adhesion of each in particular. Consequently he tries to persuade himself that he is in the true religion but he is not sure that others may also be a little in it. These last, he reckons, are as sincere as he is: they believe as he does to be in truth. It follows then that it is out of the question to impose upon others the Catholic belief or even to captivate for the exclusive gain of the Catholic Church the power of the State, which by definition must impartially ensure the advantage common to all. Consequently, Social life must be organized according to a *modus vivendi* which can be in no other way than by official neutrality and universal tolerance. Thus the lack of faith leads to "the liberty of conscience" and by it to social atheism. No longer wishing that the true religion guide and dominates politics we conclude with politics which is irreligious and anti-religious.

This is already the error which Pope Gregory XVI denounced when he wrote:

> From this infected source, this absurd and erroneous maxim, or rather from this delirious maxim by which we are to assure and guarantee to each and everyone the "liberty of conscience," indifferentism flows.

Because of his lack of faith in the Church, leaning too much towards error by his obsessive desire of conciliation and peace, the "Liberal Catholic" is moved, convulsed, and even ashamed when he is accused of intransigence and intolerance. So he locks himself within his little conscience believing that he is in total security there. I believe, for my part, that he considers himself to be in the Catholic religion. I am right, but perhaps you are not in error when you admit the Protestant or Buddhist doctrine. And then, in his great desire of unity he comes out of his private conscience, only to courageously confirm a vague Christian idealism[6] which is above the divergences of confessions, and from there he nobly elevates this Christian idealism even unto a moral social idealism which is above all religions.

Encouraged by the applause of the adversaries to the Catholic faith, he preaches the "mutual respect of religious convictions and philosophical opinions." And why should we not live, he continues in a reciprocal tolerance, in a wide and generous liberty? Let us forget the past struggles, the terrible memories of the Inquisition and terror. Let us mutually guarantee a tranquil presence in common justice, under the protection of the majestic and serenely placed State, which is beyond and outside all diverse religious confessions.

Even if the "Liberal Catholic" would use the notion of "liberty of conscience" as an argument *ad hominem* to draw every Catholic who is thus free to believe and practice the Catholic religion, over which the State has no say other than to protect her

---

[6] Regarding the Sillonists, Pope St. Pius X spoke of their "social dreams," of "irreducible idealists," of their "generous liberalism."

liberty, it would still hardly be admissible because the argument remains equivocal and dangerous, and would be, without doubt, inefficacious. However, he goes much further than this. The State, he thinks, has nothing to do with religion because it is a question of a "purely confessional" order. It is in no way political nor social, but individual. It regards each religious confession, each conscience. It comes exclusively from the interior forum, a sacred domain prohibited to the State. It follows that politics is separated from religion and therefore independent. Without doubt, the individual is held to believe and to practice the only true religion. We are reminded very rarely of this grave and primordial obligation, "supreme duty," "the most holy of all duties," wrote Pope Leo XIII. But, continues the Liberal, the State must be rigorously "neutral," essentially "secular."

Consequently, if the "Liberal Catholic" should concern himself with politics, whether it be in a newspaper or electoral posting, deputy or minister, municipal councilor or vice-prefect, or if he should become part of the administration of the State or occupy a chair of official teaching, he is obliged to turn himself inside out. There would be a side of him as a private man, very moral, pious, practicing, even communicating several times during the week, he would even be very submissive to his confessor or his parish priest; and the other side of him, a man perfectly neutral in public affairs, careful to prevent an oppression of someone else's liberty, tolerating the profession of Faith, at least under the condition of also allowing a communist demonstration, treating all religions in an absolutely equal way, practically independent of religion, the Church or God.[7]

But this is "secularism"! a perspicacious observer would object. This is to organize public life according to the requirements and exclusive gains of a determined doctrine, that of social atheism! Not at all, would our "Liberal Catholic" reply in soft agitation. You confound two distinct things: the neutrality of the state

---

[7] "These Catholics, and there are not a few, dare to limit the divine power, pretending to depend upon divine power for their own private lives, but not for their public lives. This is why they so easily converse with our enemies on the religious-political terrain. And what disasters do these compromises bring us" (Cardinal Andrieu, 1922).

which is laicized on the one hand (seen to be good) and intolerance, religious persecution and secularism on the other (seen to be bad).

Thus, he continues with wonderful eloquence. Secularism which makes of irreligion a sort of religion of the State is what we formally reprove in the name of liberty. This is a kind of clericalism coming back. We do not want this nor the likes of it. We "detest intolerance, whatever it may be and from wherever it may come"; we want liberties and liberty for everyone.

To be secular, on the contrary, equitably forms the State outside and above these diverse religious confessions; it consists in "the reciprocal independence of Church and State and the reciprocal respect in liberty." Certainly the State must never be secularist, but in the present state of profound divisions of consciences, it must be secular, that is to say, neutral. It must not be hostile to any religion, but must show its benevolent impartiality to everyone. Here we may add: such a duty would seem to be the rule of a republican government based upon popular or majority vote; an absolute government would necessarily be "clerical" in one sense or another.

In short, for that which concerns the civil and religious powers, the "Liberal Catholic" neither wants their complete unity (ancient paganism), nor the subordination of religious to the civil power (secularism), nor the domination of the religious power over the civil (theocracy and clericalism), but simply their separation in such wise as to have two independent civil powers.

If the Church rejects the union and integration of religion with a determined political party, she nevertheless also rejects the total separation of politics and religion. She wants all political parties to accept her teachings and conform their attitude to her own doctrine. She does not hide the fact that she wishes to Christianize the State in both its personnel and actions. She wishes, in the name of the rights of God and for the great benefit of all, to Christianize the State's laws and institutions.[8]

---

[8] It is by an untruthful sophism that we call it "clerical interference and domination."

The "Liberal Catholic" despises the teachings of the Church and ignores the rights of God. He continues to hold fast to the separation of the Church and State. "Questions of creed," he writes, "have nothing to do with politics. Its intrusion in this domain has already done great harm..."

The "Liberal Catholic," therefore continues preaching the separation of the Church and State, of Catholic and citizen. Because every Catholic is also a citizen, he continues, he has the right and duty to pursue the good of the State in a self determined manner. Without considering the authority of the Church, her desires, her counsels or her commandments, nay even scorning her reprimands, he may continue to pursue it. To cause the citizen to follow a certain line of conduct for whatever reason is an abuse of ecclesiastical power. One has a duty to react with all one's force.

Does he not realize that Pope St. Pius X had already most solemnly condemned this in his encyclical *Pascendi?* [9]

The State must, therefore, be separated from the Church, and the Catholic from the citizen. Every Catholic, from the fact that he is also a citizen, has the right and the duty to work for the common good in the way he thinks best, without troubling himself about the authority of the Church, without paying any heed to its wishes, its counsels, its orders—nay, even in spite of its rebukes. For the Church to trace out and prescribe for the citizen any line of action, on any pretext whatsoever, is to be guilty of an abuse of authority, against which one is bound to protest with all one's might. Venerable Brethren, the principles from which these doctrines spring have been solemnly condemned by Our Predecessor, Pius VI, in his Apostolic Constitution, *Auctorem fidei*.

Is it then surprising that one be scandalized by such a doctrine written by Catholic publishers? One such publication is

---

[9] It is strange that one should bring side by side the texts of Pius X and M. Desgrees du Lou in *Ouest-Eclair* the day after the condemnation of the Sillon: "...Let the theologian meditate upon St. Thomas...let the Bishop govern his diocese and the Pastor his parish...: It's their affair not ours. It is then also our business and not theirs, to give the politics of the *Ouest-Eclair* the direction which we judge the best and the most wise; a direction better suited to its objective and the best for our homeland and republic..."

even directed by a priest, who, it must be said, is a "Liberal Catholic." Such doctrine is even professed by those who congratulate themselves for recruiting their adherents from among Catholics, especially from among the movements for the young.

A few months ago, a young talented journalist criticized this liberal doctrine, especially concerning its foolish distinction between "secularism and secular":

> For us, the State, even according to the hypothesis, has an essential duty towards God and the form of religion which He has instituted, the Catholic Church. This "well-meaning impartiality," which places all confessions upon the same footing, and that would include those of free thought, atheists, Freemasons, even though it is preferable to persecution, remains a radical and intolerable evil.

"It is only the Catholic religion which has the right to be supported by laws and governmental authority" (Pius VII); even more so in a State where there exists a division of consciences. Sometimes, in accordance with the Church, the government would be obliged to tolerate dissident cults, not in the name of liberty, but to safeguard her common good. Fr. de la Taille writes:

> The State has the duty to recognize God, to serve Him, and, as Pope St. Pius X puts it, to safeguard the chaste alliance between Church and State. Even if there should be a great religious division like at the time of the birth of Christendom, or troubled times as at the time of the Albigensian heresy or religious wars, or even deep and profound difficulties as those of our times, the State or government always retain the duty to render to God that which belongs to Him. True, the State is not to torment consciences, but nevertheless, it is to safeguard its own. In the interest of the common good, it is not for the State to suppress or restrain the liberties enjoyed by dissident cults. But it is the State's duty to proclaim its alliance to the faith of Christ. This is so because it does not come as a mandate from a pretended sovereign people, but from the fact that the State is firstly the representative and delegate of God for the temporal well being of its subjects.

The vain incoherencies and utopian distinctions of the "Liberal Catholic" are far from the firm and well-presented doctrine of the Church regarding the notion of the religion of the State. In this doctrine the Church "requires of the State to protect the true religion, without however forcing its belief and practice." The Church quite reasonably wants the "Christian State to recognize her divine mission. It nevertheless tolerates the practice of the dissident cults which have acquired the right to this tolerance, without itself participating therein." This is the only way to respect the truth without damaging the common good, to safeguard the rights of God and the good of souls at the same time.[10]

The Democratic Ambiguity

The "Liberal Catholic" does not run dry quickly. He is a real master of confusion. It is impossible to show all the ambiguities which emanate from his teaching. There are however, two which we still wish to explain because of their importance in our day and age: These are the democratical equivocal and the common good.

It is a fact, as we have said, that the "Liberal Catholics" generally show themselves favorable to the parliamentary regimes and are today in majority devoted to democracy.

Is Democracy a superior form of government? Reason easily shows the contrary. To be convinced in this, one would simply have to consult the manuals of natural law, or to listen to the teachings of profound intellectuals of the 19th century; from Joseph de Maistre to Charles Maurras. Democracy was tentatively shown to be the best form of government; it would better assure the absolute value of the human person; it would be more apt to

---

[10] Let us be reminded of two canons concerning the Church, which was to be presented to the Fathers of the first Vatican Council:
Canon II: If anyone say that this intolerance by which the Catholic Church expels and banishes all religious sects separated from Her communion, is not commanded by divine right; or: that we can have no certainty about religious truth but only opinions and therefore, the Church must tolerate all religious sects, let him be anathema.
Canon XX: If anyone say that the supreme rule of conscience for public and social acts consists in the law of the State or in the opinion of men; or: that the judgments of the Church by which she decides what is permissible or not, do not affect these before said actions; or: that what is illicit by divine or ecclesiastical right, becomes licit in virtue of the civil right; let him be anathema.

make justice reign and to bring about the happiness of the people. Pope St. Pius X in his *Encyclical on the Sillon*, overturned these pretensions of fetish democratism in recalling the words of Leo XIII: "Justice is compatible with the three known forms of government...in this respect, democracy does not have any privilege." Pius XI repeats the common opinion in showing that "the representatives of modern governments...where...the people partake more in the direction of the State...lend themselves more easily than any other institution to the disloyal game of factions. This fact is not hard to see" (*Ubi Arcano*).[11]

Is it because the democratic form is better adapted to our country, our temperament, needs or tradition? No less proved. Even the practice of parliamentary and popular regimes seem to cause more and more a tendency to authority, to the need of unity and stability in the government.

The true reason for the infatuation of "Liberal Catholics" for democracy must be sought elsewhere. It is in the fact that democracy is a nice word which encompasses an entire philosophy, we could say, an entire religion; a liberal mysticism inherited from Luther, Rousseau and the French Revolution of 1789.

In fact, democracy is no longer what it was at the time of Aristotle, Cicero or St. Thomas Aquinas. In their time, democracy was a simple way to perceive the organization of public powers. This new democracy is an ideal of social justice, a bettering and a progressive equality of conditions. It tends towards a social state where "men become more and more conscientious and responsible while laws and governments become more and more useless and obsolete." This would result from fatal progress, the summit of a new civilization having as foundation liberty, equality and the sovereignty of the people. This will be the superior state of humanity born from the infant Middle Ages and matured through the 18th century. From hence it can guide itself without counselor or tutor, without fetter or any dependency. One is told with a great enthusiasm of this "great and majestic launch which will draw people towards democracy, that is, towards that social

---

[11] St. Thomas also thinks that democracy has few advantages and many disadvantages (*De Regimine principum* L.I C.V.).

organization which will guarantee for each individual an amplification of his rights and duties...the mature world moves towards democracy." It will finally be a perfect life in which man may dynamically live, progress even unto infinity, and in which man will develop a maximum sense of responsibility and dignity.[12]

From now on every individual and society must be formed and organized in view of the principles of this new religion. We are even told of the formation of a democratic education. There seems even to be a democratic asceticism!

Freemasonry tries to substitute Catholicism with this democratic religion. The "Liberal Catholic" protests, on the contrary, desiring to see the flowering of the evangelical doctrine. He claims: "the profound aspirations of our age leading to the dignity of man, social justice, democratic life and universal fraternity, is no problem to the Church for she finds in them the influence of her own teachings."

Finally this religion will have its own apostles, or rather fanatics. The least ardent of these will not be among the "Liberal Catholics." Willingly despising the past, caring little for the realities of the present, they live in their dream-world of the future. There they have no difficulty of reconstructing a new city upon new foundations where finally a perfect identity of virtue and happiness will be found!

It is therefore a real evolution and transformation of the word democracy. Already in 1890, Mgr. Freppel mentioned these phenomena:

---

[12] Speaking about the Sillonists, Pope St. Pius X well defined this kind of democracy: "What they call democracy is; a political and social organization founded upon...liberty (taken in the sense of the autonomy of man, first condition of his dignity), equality (in the sense of complete justice which will bring about the leveling off of all conditions, political, economical and intellectual), fraternity (which is the love of a greater good bringing authority to nil)." Such an organization must also bring about as great a participation as possible of each person in the government of public affairs "producing the only society capable of assuring the ideal of human dignity. Each citizen will be of royal dignity, each worker a master."

Here Democracy is not a form of government, but rather an anti-Christian doctrine, which has as its central aim the secularization of all laws and institutions according to the form of social atheism.

To try to Christianize such a democracy is to do the impossible and only increases dangerous confusion.[13]

Do you see the unexpected consequences that the "Liberal Catholic" causes from his equivocal teaching?

The Popes, especially towards the end of the last century and the beginning of this one, taught that the Church accepts any form of government as long as certain conditions are fulfilled. But did not Leo XIII ask French Catholics to accept their democratic Republic in view of a greater good? Evidently he spoke of the form of government, since at the same time he explicitly urged them to combat all principles which would not be in conformity with Catholic doctrine as also all legislation which would proceed from these false principles. He wished that Catholics would support the Republic (this is the means) to better combat the false principles and sectarian legislation (this is the aim), that they would adhere to the democracy as a form of government to better combat the democracy as a doctrine. In this way they would really be supporting a Christian Republic. Up to this point therefore, there is no possibility of any equivocals; he is truly speaking about a democracy as a form of government.

The "Liberal Catholic" will use this word democracy as a very convenient label to promote his liberal merchandise such as: His principles of undefined liberties which are more or less contrary to authority, his popular sovereignty, his false dignity of man,[14] his

---

[13] The temporal homeland herself will inevitably suffer in her interests if she is to be subject to such a democracy. "The Republic," wrote Fr. de la Taille in 1908, "no longer operates in France other than as a national destructive agency directed by an irresponsible Syndicate of anonymous exploiters" (*En Face du Pouvoir*, p.144).

[14] Pope St. Pius X decried this false human dignity which reads: "Man will not be man, worthy of his name, until the day in which he acquires a clear, strong, independent and autonomous conscience by which he will become master of himself, obeying himself only and thus be able to as-

bulldozing equality, his mystical progress, *etc*. This is now an altogether different democracy.

This is the way our "Liberal Catholic" thinks:

Major: Democracy (according to the philosophical and classical understanding of Aristotle, St. Thomas Aquinas and Pope Leo XIII) is a legitimate form of government. Pope Leo XIII even explicitly invited French Catholics to loyally support it.

Minor: Now we are passionately democratic (according to the understanding of Rousseau, Lamennais, Maret, Sangnier...);

Conclusion: Therefore the Church supports our efforts, or at least, she holds them as legitimate without condemning them. Let's face it, how many times has Pope Leo XIII not publicly congratulated the supporters for having obeyed his urgent advice.

What a beautiful sophism! Could one be ever more ambiguous concerning the word democracy? Such a duplicity of reasoning has allowed the "Liberal Catholics" to betray the thoughts of Pope Leo XIII. In this way they continue to accept the Republic in its constitutions, principles and legislation, supporting the form of government so as to more effectively spread their liberal dogmas. If we then attack their liberal dogmas, they accuse us of attacking their perfectly legitimate political convictions. This allows them then to spread a terrible liberal propaganda, even in the heart of Catholic movements, under the mask of civil loyalty.

---

sume the most grave responsibilities without forfeiture" (*Encyclical on the Sillon*).

* [Translator's Note.] It is important to note that following a change of circumstance and also, without doubt, having obtained more complete information, the politics of Pope Leo XIII by which he encouraged French Catholics to support their government, was slowly and discreetly being abandoned. This became a fact accomplished in 1909. (cf. Discourse of Pius X to French pilgrims, April 19, 1909 and also the reply given by Cardinal Merry del Val to Col. Keller in May of the same year). In March 1911, Cardinal Luon explained without fear of contradiction, the mind of Pope St. Pius X, that the constitutional ground had been put aside by the Pope as an element of discord and as unacceptable after a definite lack of success. From now on the religious ground was considered as the only basis of union between the Catholics of France. From that moment, there was no pontifical document issued to even suspect that the line of conduct of St. Pius X had changed.

And so, since especially those days when "Liberal Catholics" were maltreated by Pope Pius IX, they expressly sought to change their name. Today they call themselves; "Social Catholics" or "Christian Democrats." Their mentality however has not changed because their principles and attitude have not changed. Democratism authentically continues Liberalism.

Fortified with pontifical teachings, we must not cease to put people on guard against these confusions by showing the necessary distinctions. The term or name democracy, for example, could have four principle meanings:

a) Democracy in the sense of a beneficial action of the Church in favor of the different classes; this would be Christian democracy completely devoid of a political meaning. It is simply that manifestation of Catholic charity which has always been the herald of corporal and spiritual works of mercy. In this sense, all Catholics must be democratic.

b) Democracy in the sense of a government for the people, especially favorable to the lower classes, always caring for their pressing needs. In this sense, all governments, even the most absolute monarchies must be democratic. All authority, whatever may be its form, comes from God for the good of those subjected to it.

c) Democracy in the classical sense is the special form of government by which the people are called to a greater participation in the activities of public affairs. Although this form is a less perfect one, it remains legitimate like aristocracy and monarchy. In this sense all Catholics may be democratic. The determination and adaptation of this democracy in a given country will be a question of reason, experience and prudence.

d) Democracy according to the liberal sense of Rousseau, Lamennais, Maret and Sangnier, is more a general philosophy based upon the principles of 1789 as we have explained above, than a form of government. We could rather call it Democratism. No Catholic can or is allowed to be such a democrat. Every Catholic is bound to accept with the Church:

- a wisely regulated liberty, the faculty by which he may act to accomplish good;
- natural and necessary inequalities instead of tending towards the disappearance of classes;
- the true concept of authority which has its origin in God and not in the people, and its nature being to serve by commanding and not a pure service without commandment; *i.e.,* a consented authority;
- the true notion of human dignity, compatible to the humility of his condition, and not the hypertrophical exaltation of the Ego, nor the demagogical outbidding;
- the indirect subordination of the State to the Church in its required Christianization in politics and legislation;
- the social reign of Our Lord Jesus Christ, *etc...*

Therefore, according to the sense explained above, a Catholic would have either the duty, simple faculty or rigorous prohibition to be a democrat. But if he particularly wishes to be a democrat in politics, he would be obliged, even like any monarchist, to profess the integral doctrine of the Church. Given the circumstances of today, he would also be obliged to be extremely prudent and circumspect so as not to lay himself open to the errors which the modern meaning of this word draws unto itself, lest by his love for this kind of government, he espouses the mentality lurking behind it and falls for the condemnable and condemned democracy (cf. *Encyclical of Pope St. Pius X against the Sillon.*).

Conclusion

"Liberal Catholicism" or whatever name one might give it, such as "Christian Democracy" or "Social Catholicism," is a general sickness of the mind which extends to every domain, whether it be practical or theoretical. Unfortunately it is impossible to go into great detail concerning all its nuances. It suffices to recall its origin or historical development and its principle traits and mentality, particularly its doctrinal incoherency, its radically false mind, its special attitude concerning the relationships between Church and State, and the multiple ambiguities behind which it hides.

In conclusion, let us insist upon some special dangers of "Liberal Catholicism" and suggest some appropriate remedies.

The Danger of "Liberal Catholicism"

The absolute and logic of Liberalism, born out of Rationalism, produces a horror. By its bluntness it catches only a few. Those who simply hold on to the true faith and doctrine, and give an attentive ear to the Magisterium of the Church, are normally not caught.

"Liberal Catholicism," on the contrary, is much more dangerous. Its effects we have already shown: judgment becomes weak, conscience indifferent and the mind is filled with confused ideas. How can anyone conserve the immaculate tradition of the Church in a world full of degrading art and images?

Few would jump from the heights of Catholicism to the abyss of Liberalism. "Liberal Catholicism" offers and disposes the intermediary ledge to break the fall and render it insensible. As we have said once before, "if there were no nuances or middle step between truth and error, few men would have such sad courage as to take the step. They would need to descend slowly, step by step to familiarize themselves with the darkness." The gray area of "Liberal Catholicism" gives perfect opportunity to this transition between the whiteness of pure Catholicism and the pitch darkness of Liberalism.[1]

Among the conglomeration of philosophies and religions, the "Catholic Liberal" places himself between the right, representing the truth of Catholicism, and the left representing the chaos of errors. From here he has the audacity to proclaim himself in the "just middle." But, they would object, when one is on a slope, one can climb up or descend. Yes, but the "Liberal Catholic" has a perpetual tendency towards the progressive left. Logically, and by force of change, he is less and less Catholic and ever more Liberal. Since he ordinarily condescends to the weaknesses and miseries of his times, we see him normally descend towards errors, treason and apostasy. We could compare him to a fool, who wishing to save someone from falling off a precipice, stretches forth his helping hand, anchors himself on a little tuft of grass and so falls head long with the other into the abyss.

The "Liberal Catholic" does not stay close to his Mother the Church. He hardly knows her doctrines and disregards her warnings. He is far too obsessed, not with a saving apostolate, but with accommodations and conciliations which make him slide towards them. He resembles the blind man leading the blind and both fall into the pit.

He ignores the principles. By keeping silent in their regard, he ends up forgetting them, or, he is ignorant of their hierarchical order and so confounds them and ends up falsely interpreting them. Consequentially, he no longer sees clearly the difference between good and evil, the Church and sects, or even between God and Satan. He no longer possesses that intransigent and holy horror for error and evil which is the mark of a true Catholic mind. By his mentality of concessions he ends up in pure tolerance. His "broad mind" causes him no longer to consider the psychological point of view of his adversary to better reform him, nor does he judge him from the height of Catholic wisdom, but

---

[1] "The error of honest people," wrote Le Play, "are the worst of all errors."

often goes so far as to accept and admit his adversary's point of view and ends up assuming the principles which govern the errors. In this way he arrives at those "blaspheming similitudes" (Pius X)[2] between the Gospel and the Revolution, Jesus Christ and Socialism, and the Church and a certain democracy...This is how he finally comes to publish his veneration of the "immortal principles of 1789" which Pope Pius VI declared "injurious to both religion and society." Much more preoccupied with persons than with principles, with popularity than with "truth in charity," he tries more to please them by respecting their erroneous convictions, than to do them a good turn by reminding them of the hard truth which he believes, unfortunately, to be out of fashion.

He totally lacks "Catholic sense." Catholic sense simply consists of "always adhering to the sentiments and preferences of the Church, *sentire cum Ecclesia*, and of thinking and appreciating like she does even when she does not define. It seeks to obey her least impulse even if she does not command." The "Liberal Catholic" on the contrary always seeks to protect his most precious liberty in a persevering mania of always strictly limiting his "Credo" to defined truths only. The rest he leaves in his category of "free opinions." He thinks himself to be in perfect line with the Church as long as he does not hold any formal heresies. He forgets the long line of censures, from "bitter" to "erroneous," which the Church imposes upon propositions which are not agreeable to her. The "Catholic sense" may be compared to the spirit of a large family, which is the Church. The "Liberal Catholic" perverts this sense and is therefore the first to cause divisions. Of course, he blames those who criticize him. Again the "Catholic sense" is the spirit of tradition. The "Liberal Catholic"

---

[2] It is necessary to cite this passage since it so well explains to "Liberal Catholics" their error: "The exaltation of their sentiments (the leaders of the Sillon), the blind goodness of their hearts, their philosophical mysticism mixed with illuminism, have led them to a new Gospel in which they believe to have found the true gospel of the Savior. This has caused them to dare to treat Our Lord Jesus Christ with a terribly disrespectful familiarity, and because their ideas stem from the Revolution, they, without fear, blasphemingly place the Gospel and the Revolution on the same footing..."

is ignorant of Catholic tradition. He is quick to conform to the errors of today and shows little care of conforming to the eternal truths.

This mentality extends to everything. Like some sicknesses destroy the taste, the liberal sickness radically destroys "Catholic sense." Why then should we be astonished when we see "Liberal Catholics" successively uphold:

- the unreasonableness of the declaration of the dogma of the Immaculate Conception,
- of the *Syllabus*
- of pontifical infallibility
- Americanism and the supporting of Loisy (Father of Modernism)
- biblical and historical naturalism and rationalism,
- intuitive and pragmatic philosophies
- different modernisms (dogmatic, judicial, social, practical),
- the separation of Church and State,
- cultural associations,
- no resistance offered against the taking of Church property (France) nor the expulsion of religious,
- democratism (Sillon),
- unseasonableness of Holy Communion to children,
- acceptation and respect for the "secular laws,"
- the Declaration of the Rights of Man,
- the separation of politics and religion,
- Ecumenism,
- renewals in the Liturgy,
- systematic silence on the truths of eternal damnation,
- neutrality in movements,

etc., etc., etc,.

Now it is no longer difficult to understand why so many condemnations from the Church have come exclusively upon the heads of these "Liberal Catholics." It is then not surprising to see, coming from the midst of them, so many revolts and scandalous apostasies. All that we have seen above has come from the speculative and doctrinal side. Now let us look at the practical side.

In practice, the "Liberal Catholic," contrary to certain exterior appearances, lacks true charity both for his adversary whom he supports, and in regards to the true Catholic whom he despises. This is because he lacks true principles and truth. First charity goes to God and His rights. As to his neighbor, he firstly owes him the spiritual works of mercy, which has always been to teach the ignorant and not to tolerate their evils.

He lacks true prudence. Prudence looks towards its end, wants it, takes the means to attain it and seeks to truly possess it. His prudence, on the contrary, consists above all in wisely retreating. He seems to be ignorant of the "irresistible moral superiority of him who does not continually weigh his chances but goes on straight ahead."[3] His prudence and talents really consist only in self-management.

He has no character because he has no conviction. Le Play's remark fits him perfectly: "what is lacking in the men of our age is above all the strength in conduct which produces confidence in the power of truth."

He lacks a supernatural outlook and Christian sense. We have seen more than once his lack of faith and his naturalistic tendencies. This shows especially in his sermons, if he is a priest, and in his works. He seems to forget the power of God, the *virtus Dei* and places an exaggerated confidence in mean human ways. He rarely sees the supernatural aim of his actions. He forgets that these human works are to aim at the moral and religious amendment of life. Slowly he substitutes the religious sense with a vague "social sense" and puts material well-being first. He humanizes the mission of the Church and strangely belittles it.

His apostolate also necessarily takes a strange turn because of his lack of faith and Christian sense. One hardly sees his adversaries convert, or rather, one sees many perversions caused or even operated by him.[4] And why should we be surprised? Cardinal Pie writes:

---

[3] A distinguished priest used to say: "For the Catholic and Priest, to be upright is to be clever."

[4] This is especially seen when he favors among his adversaries, a progress of this spirit of independence which constitutes the foundation of his mentality. For example, in the social order, he promises an imminent

One only becomes an apostle under the condition that one strives for sanctity. The first condition of sanctity is orthodoxy. Even a great and generous ardor cannot become its substitute. We can do nothing without grace, and it will help even less if we separate grace from doctrine. Error, even when it is not culpable nor constitutes a formal sin, will prove to be a great obstacle to the fecundity of word and action of the minister of God.

It is remarkable to see just how opposed the "Liberal Catholic" is to true Catholic spirituality, which has as its foundation, an intellectual submission to God by a virginal faith, and the conformity of the will to God by humility. To this is added self abnegation, detachment, a non-compromising battle against the passions, especially pride, filial obedience, which goes even as far as the admirable and holy slavery explained by St. Louis Grignon de Montfort, or attains the "spiritual childhood" of St. Theresa of the Infant Jesus which Pope Pius XI set before our eyes as a heroic model.

The "Liberal Catholic" on the contrary aims at the enlargement of the domain of liberty, favoring the abandonment of each individual to his own inspiration or blossoming. The Holy Ghost Who thus inspires the heart of each, substitutes any exterior direction. The "passive" virtues are put aside together with the supernatural virtues, while the natural and active virtues are considered more appropriate for our present times. Both education and spirituality of the "Liberal Catholic" consist mainly in developing in man his sense of dignity, personality and responsibility.

Religion of the interior according to the Protestant mode, religion of individual liberty, religion of well-being, religion of tolerance and concessions, of the exaltation of man, of confidence in oneself, etc., in short, "broad Catholicism," this is the ideal of the "Liberal Catholic."

But is all this really Catholic?

The way the "Liberal Catholic" thinks and acts is truly very dangerous.

---

abolishment of salary-structure which he calls a type of slavery. He congratulates commoners for having acceded to the majority and so prepare for the coming of the worker's union....He does all of this without ever preaching justice, charity or a Christian acceptation of their condition.

More than being simply incoherent in his doctrine or having a lack of faith, he stubbornly holds fast to his little conceptions. Just as under the mask of moderation he hides his headstrong sectarianism, so under his "broadness of mind" he hides his evil narrowness of mind. If he should direct a movement or organize a congress, or institute a school of sociology, he will turn only to those of the same mind and taste as he. If he writes a history book, directs a journal or produces a manual, he will again praise only those who are normally not praised by the Church.

The "Liberal Catholic" is very dangerous:

Under the banner of the Apostolate, he corrupts Catholic thinking, without enlightening or winning over his adversaries. On the contrary, he consolidates their positions. When Pope Leo XIII encouraged the support of the Democratic Republic in France, or when Pope Pius XI condescended to a dishonest government, these same popes did not forget to vigorously remind everyone of the necessary principles and even solemnly condemned Rationalism, Liberalism and secularism. Practical kindness will naturally flow from a firm doctrine. Under all kinds of fantastic pretexts, (not to compromise the Church, nor upset the adversary, or to gain his sympathy) the "Liberal Catholic" systematically passes the principles over in silence, if of course he does consider these catholic truths and the rights of God at all. "While he flatters himself for attracting these bad people on their own terrain," writes Mgr. de Ségur, "he himself slips and falls on the battlefield," swallowing their evil ways.[5]

The "Liberal Catholic" is very dangerous:

By keeping silent on behalf of the principles, or in diminishing truths by substituting limp salutary doctrine with a cloud of equivocals, he causes error to become amiable, evil acceptable, and he himself, just about incurable. As we have said before; "just ideas cause a barricade against evil practices, and even when these cannot prevent it, they still render these practices remediable. False ideas on the contrary, cause evils from which we never re-

---

[5] Nothing is more acceptable or flattering to the "Liberal Catholic" than the equivocal applause and congratulations of the adversaries of the Church.

pent nor even have remorse," nor are we even conscious of them. Instead of ranking among Catholics who see evil and know how to denounce them, *hi viderunt mala quae fiebant in populo Juda et in Jerusalem* (I Macc. 2:6), they merit the anathema of the prophet; *Vae qui dicitis malum bonum et bonum malum* (Is. 5: 20).[6] When we thus call good good and evil evil, nothing is lost. Conscientious horror of evil and error can help for prevention as well as cure. But when evil is called good or error is sought to be justified, then there is no longer even hope for salvation.[7]

The "Liberal Catholic" is very dangerous:

By perpetually seeking to operate an impossible accommodation of truth and error, good and evil, pure doctrine and pretended exigencies of hypothetical sciences, doubtful compromises and firm judgments, or substituting principles with expediency, he causes minds to be clouded in confusion. This causes them to lose the appreciation of rectitude. It causes falseness of mind, breaks down convictions and courage, and renders an inefficacious resistance to evil which is by now hardly perceived anyhow.

In this world, the Church is essentially "militant" because of the inevitable battle for truth against error, for order against anarchy, the Christian city against the antichristian city, God against Satan. Conciliation or peace is only possible through the triumph of the truth of Jesus Christ. The Catholic army marches united for the salvation of souls and for the triumph of Jesus Christ, in truth, animated by charity and under the command of the Pope and Bishops. In this army, the "Liberal Catholic" instigates trouble and causes division, obscures the banner, hides away, makes a pact with the enemy and even ends up deserting and becoming a traitor.

An enemy or declared adversary is by far less dangerous than these false friends, these traitors, or at least these milksops who "have the eternal function of opening the door to the enemy, stabbing good Catholics in the back, and destroying every effort

---

[6] "Woe to him who calls evil good and good evil"
[7] Let us add in passing that the "Liberal Catholic" is quick to allude to the perverse intentions of Catholics, while he always considers the adversary's intentions as pure. This causes their errors, or as he calls them "partial truths," to become more amiable.

of converting souls," who hold tight to the conciliation in obscuring evil, in keeping silent or even erasing truth, and in blackening the salutary good.

"Liberal Catholics" are as dangerous in what they say as in what they do not say. They keep a calculated silence, and continue in their obstinacy of not speaking to certain persons concerning certain things, while they praise certain personalities without discretion or necessary reservations so as to make authorities of these and so trick the gullible reader. All of this is for no other reason than to consolidate the position of the adversary and to sow discord among Catholics, breaking thereby their resistance and preventing their victorious advancement.

The "Liberal Catholic" is very dangerous:
St. Pius X insistently invited Catholics:

> ...to take confidence in themselves in a frank and energetical affirmation of the principles of Christian law. They must remain on Catholic terrain instead of allowing themselves into the den of illusions and deceptive alliances, or to hope in a false peace, and must not allow themselves to become impersonalised by the opposition which is "Liberal Catholicism."

The true Catholic seeks to strengthen Catholic forces by means of a greater union and clear principles. Once this is established, he goes ahead and tries to find a temporal and loyal alliance with a predetermined aim, and this with men of order, where Catholicism will suffer no diminution even though she might claim only a certain part of her rights. But the "Liberal Catholic" is hypnotized by quantity and the desire to please the "left." He steadily destroys the Catholic program, keeping silent regarding her name as if he sees in her a "damaged and smuggled commodity" (Pius X), and seeks, in the night of confusion which he causes by his carefully hidden equivocal "liberal" etiquette, a superficial agreement which is beneficial only to the enemy.[8]

---

[8] The words of L. Veuillot are true even today: "We perhaps have lost more truths through good people who have lost courage to say them, than errors which evildoers have multiplied....It is not religion which you make amiable, but your own person, and because of this you fear the loss of love and end up losing courage of being true. They indeed praise you, but, for what? For your silence and denials."

The "Liberal Catholic" is very dangerous:

Both in doctrine and practice these wise, prudent and realist "Liberal Catholics" facilitate the trespassing of the enemy and permit him an inglorious victory, simply because it was an effortless victory. "There is nothing which renders greater audacity among evil men," wrote Pope Leo XIII, "than the weakness of the good." By their mania for expediency, pretension of following the times, fear of announcing the truths which hurt, "Liberal Catholics" falsify everything from truth to liberty, authority, charity and prudence, bringing themselves to dangerous accommodations, most scandalous prevarications and shameful capitulations.

These Catholics are nearly always defeatists. They want to suppress persecution by refusing to fight. They calumniate and blaspheme against a force they know not how to place nor have the courage to use. Thanks to their consummated "wisdom" and skill in tactics, the enemy, continuing to advance, reduces unceasingly the realm of what is possible.

Pope Pius XI repeated what was said by Pope Leo XIII:

> Perhaps we are to attribute this disadvantage to the slowness and timidity of the good who resist the enemy with softness. The adversaries thus draw to themselves an overdose of temerity and audaciousness. The faithful must therefore understand that they are to fight with courage and always under the banner of Christ the King (*Croix*, December 31, 1925).

> Fr. de la Taille formulated the two systems of union, the Liberal and the Catholic, in the following way: "The question is whether Catholics should fuse together in one body with a mass of certain unbelievers and march under the same banner which will evidently not be the banner of Catholic principles but the only one having a chance to be hoisted by the generality of unbelievers susceptible to support us, and that would be the Liberal flag..." Would it not be preferable for believers to stick together under their own banner and then contract temporal alliances with unbelievers while these last remain under theirs. "Such coalitions would not exact common principles: Concordant interests as diverse as their ultimate aims, would then suffice....The choice then would be between the integrity of Catholic principles on the one side, and the presumed number of adherents on the other." Is it certain that a loyal alliance without any dangerous fusion would not attract numbers?

The "Liberal Catholic" is very dangerous:
On the one hand, they take refuge in confusion, being masters in the art of ambiguities and equivocals, and since their errors are rarely clear and formal, but rather of half-measure, they easily slip through the fingers. On the other hand they are very active, very intriguing, ordinarily profluent in speech, abundant and loud. One finds them in every institute and publication, in the press, Parliament, corridors and anti-chambers, even, and especially, the highest. They are normally always favored by governments for their services rendered or to be rendered. We cannot deny it, they make much noise and do much evil.

Having said this, we will no doubt be called things like "venomous sophists," "caterers of the Inquisition," "theologians in the clouds" and other amiable names which are certainly pleasing to no one.

Here are the thoughts of Pope Pius IX which he expressed in great sadness to the pilgrims from Nevers, France (June, 1871):

> What afflicts your country and prevents it from receiving the blessings of God, is this mixture of principles. I will tell you what it is, I will not be silent: It is not the Commune of Paris that I fear but this terrible politics which is Catholic Liberalism....This game of hide-and-seek is the real scourge of your country and destroyer of Religion. Of course one is to practice charity and to do whatever is possible to bring back these lost sheep. This however does not mean that one should share their opinions.[9]

Two years later, Pope Pius IX replied to a Catholic community of Orleans, France, by means of a brief:

> Although you are obliged to wage a war against impiety, you have a greater battle against a certain group of friends made up of men imbued with this ambiguous doctrine. They may indeed reject the extreme consequences of errors, but they retain and obstinately nourish the principal germ. In this, they do not want

---

[9] After having called to mind this discourse of Pope Pius IX, Cardinal Andrieu added (1922): "It is time to put an end to this idol of Liberalism which has so many adorers, and who, even at this moment, work furiously, under the pretext of a sacred union and religious peace, to reconcile Catholics with laws justly condemned by papal encyclicals, as assailants of the rights of God and the divine institution of the Church."

to embrace the whole truth, nor do they completely reject it. Thus they continue to interpret the teachings of the Church so as to make it conform to their own ideas.

A little while later, yet another brief to a Catholic circle of Quimper:

> Your adherents have certainly not taken to disobedience as have the enemies of the Church and the Holy See, since it is precisely against them that they have fought. They will however find a very dangerous path towards error in these so-called liberal opinions which are received by so many honest and pious Catholics. Such opinions would cause even religion and authority to draw souls to them and thus incline them to very pernicious opinions. Warn therefore, Venerable Brother (Bishop of Quimper), the members of this Catholic Association. On numerous occasions we attacked liberal opinions, and yet, it was not those who hate the Church that we had in mind. It is useless even to mention these. It was those who conserved and sustained this hidden virus of liberal principles, whom we had in mind. They have caressed these principles under the pretext that they do not thereby infect a manifest evil nor is it dangerous to religion. But these people very easily inject and propagate the seeds of the revolution from which the world has had much to suffer.

In this same year of 1873, we read in a brief to a Catholic circle of Milan:

> Even though the children of this world are more clever than the children of light, their traps (the enemies of the Church) would have so much less success if it were not for so many who hold out a helping hand, and still call themselves Catholic. Yes, unfortunately, there are those who seem to wish to march with our enemies and go out of their way to establish an alliance between the light and the darkness, between justice and iniquity. They do so by means of these doctrines which we call "Catholic Liberalism." Making use of these most pernicious errors, they flatter secular power when it invades the spiritual forum and force souls to respect, or at least, to tolerate most evil laws, as if it were never written that one cannot serve two masters. These are more dangerous and deadly than declared enemies, because they support their efforts without being noticed, perhaps not even realizing it themselves. Because they remain within the extreme limit of formally condemned opinions, they show a certain sign of apparent integrity and unreproachable doctrine, convincing

thereby imprudent amateurs who support conciliation, and mislead honest souls who would have revolted against a declared error. In this way they divide souls, break asunder unity and weaken the forces which were destined to be united in their combat against the enemy...

Again in 1873, Pope Pius IX wrote in a brief to the President of the Federation of Catholic circles in Belgium:

> What we praise most of all in this religious enterprise of yours, according to what has been told us, is your hostility against the principles of "Liberal Catholicism" which you are trying as best you can, to eradicate from the minds of men. Those imbued with these principles, declare, it is true, their love and respect for the Church. They even seem to consecrate their talents and works for her defense, but none the less, they also continue to pervert the mind and doctrines of the Church. These follow the inclination of their own minds and render either to Caesar or to those who have invented rights in favor of this false liberty. They think it to be absolutely necessary to follow this course in order to remove all dissensions, to conciliate the Gospel with the progress of today's society and so to reestablish order and tranquillity, as if light can coexist with the darkness, or as if the truth would remain when violence is done to her by changing her true signification and by stripping her of her stable inherent nature.
>
> This insidious error is more dangerous than open enmity, because it is covered with a special veil of zeal and charity. Thus by taking care to separate simple souls from it, you will extirpate this deadly root of discord and will then efficaciously work to produce and sustain a union between upright souls.

To attack these doctrines is indeed to divide, but so as to be united under the "unique sound of the bell."

Again in 1874, we read in a brief to the editors of *La Croix* in Bruxelles: The Holy Father congratulates them for their battle "especially against "Liberal Catholicism" which seeks to conciliate light and darkness, truth and error." Pope Pius IX continues:

> Without doubt you have begun a hard and difficult battle because these pernicious doctrines which open the door to all kinds of impiety, are even now violently supported by those who praise themselves for helping the pretended progress of civilization and

by those who exteriorly profess the faith but do not truly have her spirit. They ostentatiously speak everywhere about peace, while they know not even the way to peace. At the same time they draw to themselves many people who are seduced by the love of ease.

This last remark is certainly very admirable in its fine and firm psychology. It partly explains the success of "Liberal Catholicism," which flatters the common dispositions of man's fallen nature, his secret pride, his disdain for authority, confidence in self, and horror of struggle. In strengthening these dispositions, he creates: "a state of mind mildly satanic, carefully unsubmitted and opposed to God."

In another brief of February 1875 to the members of the conferences of St. Vincent de Paul of Angers, France, he wrote:

> Persevere in the faith...and never allow yourselves to be deterred from your goal whether it be by the many traps of error or the subtle and sweet discourses of those who take confidence in their own wisdom, and use for their own end such or such a doctrine of the Church. These same believe to have found some kind of middle term by which they seek the solution to the never ending conflict between truth and error. They claim to have finally found it in a mutual embrace. They think that they are being very prudent by neither following the one nor the other. They fear that the truth will disturb error, and that error would go beyond the limits which they so foolishly have assigned to it.

Finally in December of 1876, Pius IX wrote a brief to the editors of a Catholic newspaper of Rodez:

> We certainly do approve your endeavor to defend and explain the decisions of our *Syllabus*, especially those points which condemn the so-called "Catholic Liberalism," which has a large number of adherents among honest men. This error seems to be close to the truth and thus becomes very dangerous since it so easily deceives those who are not on their guard, and, because it unperceivebly and secretly destroys the Catholic mind, it greatly reduces Catholic strength while increasing that of the enemy's.
>
> To be sure, there will be many who will accuse you of imprudence and that your work is untimely. But because the truth displeases many and is the cause of irritation among those who obstinately remain in error, it must never be judged as imprudent or

precocious. On the contrary, the greater and more universal the evil to be combated, the more timely and prudent it will be. Otherwise we would have to conclude that the gospel herself was most imprudently and precociously proclaimed, since it was done at a time when religion, laws and morals of all nations were directly opposed to it. This battle will indeed cause you to be blamed and receive scorn and hateful accusations, but the One who brought the truth to the world prophesied to his disciples that they would be hated for His Name's sake.

Let us add to this. If modern man has left the cradle and become mature in order to speak that democratic-liberal jargon of his, he should be more capable than ever to support the weight of truth. This is then certainly not the time for silence.

Such declarations coming to us from on high, confirm our reflections, judgments and attitudes. But, to belittle their value, they, the "Liberal Catholics," claim that these briefs are not counted among the most solemn statements of the Vicar of Christ! Cardinal Pie replies:

> Without doubt even though they come from among his private letters, the personages addressed are not simple individuals, but rather Catholic associations whom the Vicar of Christ is instructing in doctrine. The contents of these letters are developments of documents already sent in the past to the episcopate. These briefs are explicit and motivated in their condemnations of religious liberty. One would have to be truly pertinacious to try to conciliate it with orthodox Catholicism (*Works*, VII, 567).

The bishops of Ecuador, reunited in the council of Quito (1885) wrote a collective letter which states:

> As for us, we have little fear for the ferociousness and violence offered by absolute radicalism, stark Liberalism,...Freemasonry...What we certainly fear most of all is "Catholic Liberalism," this pernicious pest, this vacillating politics, disguised hangman, more evil than the Commune of Paris, or as Pope Pius IX often put it,...this most evil error...slowly corrupting the heart, clouding the mind and finally causing the loss of souls. It ends with the ruin of Religion and nation...

Worse indeed than evil men, for these last have made martyrs, but the "Liberal Catholics" prepare the way to the apostasy of nations.

Even though this sect of "Liberal Catholics" has changed their name, they most certainly have not changed their attitude. They continue to proclaim the same principles, the same personalities, the same practices. The Bishop of Coutances wrote in 1910:

> What a terrible evil this system ("Liberal Catholicism") has done us! It is this evil which has destroyed the mind, shaken convictions and broken down strength. It is this error which has preached the necessity of concessions and given such audaciousness to error and sectarian impiety. It is this error which, under the pretext of avoiding greater evils, has demanded that truth renounce her rights. And yet, it is only the truth that can save us. Where in the world would we be today if the apostles were liberals?

At the same time, Rev. Fr. Barbier, well-known critic of Liberalism, and hated much for this by the liberal "charitans," wrote, after having cited the brief of Pope Pius IX, which we cited above:

> Whoever has read these strong words attentively, cannot possibly reject the fact that they mean literally what they say and that they refer to the state of mind which is so very common among today's Catholics. With what seriousness does it not teach the right to criticize and the duty to fight this error! "Liberal Catholicism" has again lifted its head, and holds it higher now than in the time of Pope Pius IX. We see it in every domain. It discreetly destroys the principles of discipline, it exhales a spirit of tolerance which frustrates the most indispensable convictions. It cultivates a synthetic hope of conciliation and sacrifices the absolute duty of resistance. It preaches a submissionism (an improper love for sectarian government) which it disguises under the name of fidelity to the traditional teaching of the Church. It ignores the principles of Christian law and professes an accommodation to the new law and believes it to be wise politics to renounce all privileges of the Church, of course, without Her consent. These things it does by audaciously covering everything by the name of fidelity to the Church's instructions...

Thus in short, the "Liberal Catholic" is particularly dangerous: This has been abundantly proved, both by authority and from its very nature. Far from being a simple superficial danger, it has become a most grave danger since it has even attained the intellectual elite, diffusing deep into traditional ideas of authority and order, at least among the masses, who are steadily being perverted by the liberal Catholic press.

"Liberal Catholicism" is for us Catholics the greatest obstacle to the reign of the sweet, adorable and necessary yoke of Christ the King over every individual and above all, over every society.[10] From the point of view of the individual, this Liberalism prides man in his false dignity, and prepares him in his revolt against all authority. But above all, it injects in every society the false dogma of the "liberty of conscience" through neutrality and secularism even unto universal secularism and social atheism which are the greatest evils of our modern times. It is now, therefore, the time to vigorously react and seek to apply true remedies which will heal us from this devastating sickness.

Remedies to "Liberal Catholicism"

These democratic Liberals are similar to those little bugs that come to you in the darkness of the night but disappear when light comes. They fear the honest and loyal exposition of truth and order. The first remedy against "Liberal Catholicism" would be to denounce them, to expose their illusions and the weakness of their conduct. Let us not try to harbor too much hope in converting them, but firstly to impede them by destroying the authority that they have usurped and abused.

More Positive Remedies

To repeat once again, the "Liberal Catholic" lacks practical prudence because he lacks speculative wisdom. He has no idea how to use the "hypothesis" because he is ignorant of the re-

---

[10] Concerning the whole of "Liberal Catholicism," we can say what Pope Pius X said of the Sillon: "...[these] will henceforth only form a miserable confluence of a large movement of apostasy, organized in all countries for the establishment of a universal church which will have neither dogmas, hierarchy, rules of spirit nor limits to the passions, and who, under the pretext of liberty and the dignity of man, will bring into this world, if it can succeed, the legal rule of deceit and force as well as the oppression of the weak, the suffering and those who work."

quirements and light of the "thesis." He is much more preoccupied with a "largeness of mind" than with a "sublime view." He lacks a just perspective, a profound notion of universal order which alone is capable of regulating action, and determining and measuring appreciations.

Considering its profound essence, we could define Liberalism as: "a system which pretends to justify the deregulated practice of liberty by the theoretical overturning of values." Retaining a certain proportion, this definition can also be applied to the so-called "Catholic Liberalism."

By restoring and reestablishing order and the hierarchy of values, we can ordain, or "moralize" liberty and determine its rational use. This is why the first and most urgent remedy for an intellectual sickness would be an intellectual remedy, which is to return to true wisdom and true principles. In his encyclical in which he so wonderfully spoke about liberty, Pope Leo XIII wrote:

> And if we are to find a remedy, we will find it in the sane doctrine of the Church, by which alone we can be confident in attaining the conservation of order, and through it, a guarantee of true liberty. These doctrines, are marvelous virtues by which to heal the wounds which are causing our age to suffer so, these immense and innumerable wounds which are mostly the effect of those proclaimed liberties by which men have believed to obtain happiness and glory, and which, in place of good and healthy fruits, have destroyed these high hopes and produced bitter and rotten fruit....The defense of the Christian name imperatively demands that everyone give a unanimous and constant recognition to the doctrines and teachings of the Church. Also, everyone is to guard themselves from the scheme of false doctrines, and a frailty, which is greater than truth allows in her resistance against error.

Where do we find truth and wisdom? Firstly in philosophy and particularly in metaphysics, which is the supreme wisdom in the natural order. Most of the great errors in theology, law and morality come from principles of false philosophies. "It is by philosophy and vain subtleties that the mind of the faithful of Christ are often tricked" (St. Paul). Philosophy has a great influence on either good or bad. "It is from her," wrote Pope Leo XIII, "that the wise direction of sciences depends." We seek therefore the true philosophy, and follow the Church who invites us to the "common" doctor, St. Thomas Aquinas, and to his most faithful interpreters (cf. *Aeterni Patris, Studiorum Ducem*, the 24 theses). In this philosophy we will be protected against the most dangerous errors spoken of by Pope St. Pius X: "It will be gravely detrimental to deviate from the metaphysical principles of St. Thomas Aquinas."

It is this philosophy which gives us a profound knowledge of the natural order, and shows us what to think about the world, man and God. It offers a solution to the problem of our origin and the value of ideas, and gives us the necessary principles of general morality and the natural law. It is this philosophy which best prepares us to receive and understand the supernatural order.

Supernatural wisdom can be obtained from the theology of St. Thomas Aquinas, the Magisterium of the Church and from the most pure sources, to which She, the Church, will lead us.

This theology in turn will teach us what we are to believe regarding the Holy Trinity, creation, the supernatural elevation of man, original sin, the Incarnation, Redemption and sanctification. It will teach us things concerning supernatural grace, nature, necessities, efficacious means to acquire these, prayer and the sacraments. It will show us the aim in life and the law by which we can obtain it. In this way we will obtain our true dignity. Enlightening each step, it will securely guide our uncertain conscience, by demonstrating with great precision, the duties of every moment.

Philosophy and theology in turn inspire and direct two great, but more humble sciences, which pertain more directly to our actions; those of the natural and supernatural law. Liberalism, it seems, has ravaged these sciences more than any other. Christian law disappeared with these new liberties. The natural law is no longer even taught in schools. If it is mentioned as an "introduction to the study of law," it is done in a way which is totally incoherent or biased. Thus it causes an even greater confusion and disorder in the contemporary mind. Pope Pius XI wrote:

One of the principle causes of the chaos in which we live today, is found in the grave fact that law and authority have been undermined. This happened the day in which men refused to acknowledge God as creator and master of the world, and source of all law and authority (*Ubi Arcano Dei*).

Let us then not be surprised to find strange and false thoughts among professors of law, lawyers, advocates, etc., who have indulged in the study of modern law and the "new law." Given our situation in modern democracy, these fabricators of law have an enormous influence, and are more than often malicious.

Even in our seminaries we have all too often neglected these studies of natural and Christian law. How many priests have fallen in this dangerous domain so full of errors! These evils are:

> ...presented in an enticing language which veil the sweeping ideas and equivocal expressions under the ardor of sentiment and resounding words which inflame hearts and seduce them so as to become most evil causes (Pius X, *Encyclical against the Sillon*).

We must return, with great urgency, to the serious study of natural and supernatural law which harmoniously governs the liberty of both society and the individual.

The natural law teaches us the fundamental obligations of every man to strive towards God as his last end. It points out our fundamental duty which is founded upon the superior law of God, source of our dignity and foundation of all our laws. It provides us with precise notions on moral liberty, law, authority and their relationships. It accurately describes the relationship between God and our rights and duties, between ourselves and others in the circumstances which God placed us.

Beginning from the fact of our elevation to the state of grace, the supernatural law reminds us that we cannot go to God by another way than through Jesus Christ and His Church. In particular, the public law of the Church instructs us about her nature as a perfect society, her divine origin, her supernatural end and her relationship with individuals and societies. These are indispensable notions which regulate our actions. In this way we begin to better understand the necessity of christianizing States, institutions and legislation, as well as individuals and the urgency of bringing all nations under the yoke of Christ the King.

History also has a profound influence upon the formation or deformation of the mind. Too often we have left this subject in the hands of the Rationalists and Protestants, whose mentality necessarily besmears the estimation of events and men. Indeed, time and time again, we perceive the "Liberal Catholic" consider, in a semi-rationalistic or strongly twisted mind,[11] either the early history of the Church, or the Church in the Middle Ages. Oh how much we stand in need of strong and upright Catholics who are ready to reform the many false judgments in history, which today are found cover to cover in journals, manuals and even large scientific works.

Alas, the "Liberal Catholic" mind can only deceive and be deceived. Normally his formation in theology and philosophy, his ignorance concerning the rights of the Church, together with his liberalism, already puts a just and serious suspicion upon his teachings.

> To judge history wisely, especially the history of the Church, one must possess the necessary sciences so as to see the action of God in this world, the fact of revelation, the establishment of the supernatural order and the resistance by which the evil spirit labors against the work of redemption. These were the blueprints which guided the great historians of the past (Cardinal Merry del Val to Mgr. Delassus, October 23, 1910).

Following the example of people like St. Augustine or Bossuet, the Catholic sense will help the historian to see through the mist of imperfections in society, and the work of God which continues despite all obstacles. Such a sense will cause him to see everything from the single and exact point of view, God, Who governs the world with an infinite wisdom in view of the salva-

---

[11] In this frame of mind, they think, for example, that the practice of the Inquisition or the question of privileges were really pernicious for the Church. They would wish to give the Church a wide liberty which she will generously share with all sects instead of this narrow liberty which she claims for herself only, under the pretext of being the sole possessor of the truth.

tion of souls, and obtains as such, notwithstanding the evil of evildoers, the degree of glory which was fixed from all eternity.

Philosophy, dogmatic and moral theology, natural law, public law of the Church, history...these are the principle sciences, which, if studied in a truly Catholic way, will bring about the knowledge of the objective order of all things, the natural and supernatural plan of God, and the exact hierarchy of values. This will assure the rectitude of desires. They will regulate the indocile liberty and show the true code of every Catholic action. These sciences are even more necessary to priests and Catholic laymen who devote their time to social works. Pope St. Pius X complained about the founders of the Sillon who were not "sufficiently armed with historical science, sane philosophy and solid theology, so as to confront difficult social problems without peril." Purity of intention, generosity, ardor and eloquence will never replace solid doctrine.

In his great wisdom, Pope St. Pius X recommended that Bishops appoint priests at the head of active Catholic works, who are:

> ...active and thoughtful, holding doctorate degrees in philosophy and theology and perfectly possessing the science of history...

To this he added:

> Moreover these priests must not allow themselves to be led into the abyss of contemporary opinions by the mirage of a false democracy. Neither must they employ the language of the enemies of the Church nor give ear to their emphatic and unreal promises...

All too often we find at the head of these "works" and Catholic associations, laymen or even priests, who may be very zealous, but lack sufficient formation, and are therefore incapable of giving to those confided to their care, safe directions and warnings against danger. On the contrary, these often end up leading souls astray by their imprudent councils or indiscreet choice of preachers, books or brochures.

Let us return to the subject concerning the "incredible disorder" of the liberal mind. It is only by returning to the integral truth, that we may hope to restore order into this mind. Once this mind is rectified, it will be easy for us to act with proportionate charity, prudence and force. It will be by the light of truth that the mind will be safeguarded. The mind will love her and know how to safeguard her intact and affirm her with courage.

In a most admirable passage, Leo XIII reminds us of the necessity of fighting for the truth:

> There are those who wish to prevent us from openly opposing the triumph of the all-powerful injustice, for fear that our adversaries will become upset. These people, are they for the Church or against Her? We do not know. There is nothing as powerful as to allow evil to advance. These are our enemies, whose plan it is (and do not even hide, but speak it abroad) to annihilate, if possible, the true religion, the true Catholic religion. To succeed, they recoil from nothing; they know full well that the intimidation of good souls will simplify their aim. Are we therefore to play their game so as not to stop them? Are we to join them in the prudence of the flesh totally disregarding the militant obligation of a Christian?
>
> To desist or keep silence in the face of such a clamor against the truth, is either pure weakness or a hesitation in the faith. In both cases, one would greatly dishonor God. The salvation of one's soul and that of others would be put in grave danger since such an action would be to work for the enemies of the faith, because there is nothing that so encourages the audacity of evildoers, as the weakness of good people....Let us add: Christians are born to fight...

Pope St. Pius X wrote:

> The duty of every Catholic is to unquestionably and religiously fulfill, firmly safeguard and profess without timidity,[12] both in private and in public life, the principles of Christian truths taught by the Magisterium of the Catholic Church...[Persuaded that]...error is approved by non-resistance, and truth is suffocated by not defending her.

We stand firm and reject the false pretexts which inspire a false prudence and a veritable feebleness.

---

[12] "Valiantly to serve God" said L. Veuillot.

First pretext: The hope of gaining the good will of others.

"Grave indeed is the error of those who think that they do the Church a good turn, and that they work for the good of souls, when they allow themselves to use a worldly prudence of wide concessions in the vain hope of thus winning the good will of their friends in error. In fact, all they do is put their souls in grave danger of damnation. Truth is one and undivisible, eternally the same and never submitted to the caprices of times."

Second Pretext: Human Prudence.

"Catholics are bound to zealously defend and protect the rights of the Church. There are some, however, who obey human prudence and so end up taking a stance against the Church, or show themselves timid and scared in their actions. This conduct easily leads to grave dangers."

Third Pretext: The desire for peace.

"Still worse is the error by which a vain hope for peace is sought after, since, by a pact with the world, the rights and interests of the Church are unjustly reduced and sacrificed for the sake of particular interests. Since when can we have an agreement between the light and darkness, between Christ and the Devil?"

Fourth Pretext: Charity misrepresented.

"Catholic doctrine teaches us that the first duty of charity is not in the tolerance of erroneous convictions, however sincere they might be, nor in theoretical or practical indifference regarding our brothers who have fallen into vice, but in the zeal for their intellectual and moral amendment as well as for their material needs."

In short, we must have a greater confidence in God and in His divine grace than in our miserable human ways. Thus, we will proclaim the rights of God, Jesus Christ and the Church. Thus we will strive without end, in both our private and public lives, for the restoration of all things in Christ and finally obtain the peace of Christ in the reign of Christ.

Dangers and Abuse of Words

After having shown the conditions of correct ideas, let us, in coming to an end, point out a danger which comes from the abuse of words themselves.

The "Liberal Catholic" loves ambiguous terms and confusion of ideas. It is in this "imposture of words" that he mixes the principles and violates the "virginal chastity of truth," according to the words of St. Hilary of Poitiers. This is the way by which he both tricks himself and his gullible neighbors.

It has been a great weakness for Catholics to adopt, far too often, and without making any distinctions, the words and formulas of the adversary. Under the pretext that we can better understand each other, Catholics often end up swallowing the sense and even the principles of the adversary. Fr. Barbier wrote:

> "Liberal Catholics" and Christian democrats have been the cause of great scandal...because they have induced their neighbors into error by means of their ambiguous talk. They sowed confusion and doubt, mistrust and the weakening of the faith of the simple by an attachment to these formulas which are the passports to dangerous ideas.

We praise ourselves as talented, when we use the words and expressions of our adversaries, but unfortunately, we end up falling into their trap. Listen rather to the grave warnings given to us by truly prudent men of competent authority:

Louis Veuillot:

> The betraying of words complete the ruin of principles in a secretly tainted mind.

Le Play:

> The incessant abuse of undefined words plunges the mind into a shameful inertia...This phraseology lulls the mind to sleep in error and indefinitely retards its reform...Only when we will have rid ourselves of these brutal expressions, will we again be able to take hold of our intellectual faculties...

Cardinal Pie:

> These badly defined words, placed in a deceiving envelope are received by a whole generation who end up accepting them as

absolute axioms, and yet they are in reality, completely devoid of truth.

Again the same Cardinal says:

> We have nothing to hope for from these empty and hollow words, full of vague and resounding banalities...These expressions of double meaning upon which the passions grow and the reason tries her best to explain, but the passions hold tight to the text while it disregards the commentary.

Ollé-Laprune, to whom "Liberal Catholics" often refer, writes:

> In the world of intellectual anarchy, one of the first remedies for two opposing parties, would be that every orator and thinker take a resolution never to speak in any way other than by good erudition. There are many ideas today, or, I could say better, formulas and words which are used all over and accepted everywhere, and yet without control. What a service would we render to people if we reduce the number of these vague expressions!

We have already cited Pope St. Pius X, speaking about the Sillon:

> An enticing language which veils the wave of ideas and ambiguous expressions under the ardor of sentiment. These resounding words inflame the hearts and are the seducing causes of great evil.

Pope Pius XI most strongly urged Catholics not to use "equivocals and confusing terms."

All these simply reiterate what St. Paul had already said to his disciple St. Timothy, that he should avoid "vain talk," "vain and profane discourses," and solemnly terminating, he says:

> I charge thee before God and Jesus Christ,...preach the word, be instant in season, out of season, reprove, entreat, rebuke in all patience and doctrine. For there shall be a time when they will not endure sound doctrine, but according to their own desires they will heap to themselves teachers, having itching ears, and will indeed turn away their hearing from the truth, but will be turned into fables. But be thou vigilant, labor in all things, do the work of an evangelist...

Thus we will do this work. We promise in faith, patience, charity and with force, so that by plain concepts and clear language, we may bring souls to the whole truth for the salvation of souls and for the greater glory of the immortal King of Nations and all ages, Our Lord Jesus Christ.